MW01298378

Missing Pieces
Mending the Head Injury Family

Missing Pieces

Mending the Head Injury Family

Marilyn Colter

ColterWorks

Copyright 2015 Marilyn Colter

All rights reserved, including the right to reproduce this book or portions thereof in any form. No part of this text may be reproduced, transmitted, downloaded, decompiled, reverse engineered or stored in or introduced into any information storage and distribution system, in any form or by any means without the express written consent of the author, except in the case of short (less than 30 words) reviews.

Published by Colterworks

Here's what people say about *Missing Pieces*

"The gutsiest, most compassionate, most on-target advice ever for the head injury family."
—BRAIN TECHNOLOGIES PRESIDENT DUDLEY LYNCH, FLORIDA

"Bless you, over and over! I have no memory of what I wrote when I ordered your book. But I knew I needed help after my husband's brain injury. Many times I've held your book close to my chest with the feeling that here is someone who understands. Many of our incidents are similar; it shocked me. My 'health and sanity' are at a low ebb but thanks to your help both of us will be better tomorrow. I read your book with a pencil in hand and am anxious to reread it. "
—BI FAMILY MEMBER CONNIE H., TEXAS

"Your book is sensitizing me even more and helping me to understand a little bit better. I am a rehab counselor and people with head injuries are always difficult for us too. We wish we had better answers, services, etc. I have bought the book for myself and plan to use it as a resource for others."
—REHAB COUNSELOR LINDA C., CALIFORNIA

"I would strongly recommend reading this book if you are involved with a family struggling with brain injury. The book would be even more valuable if you are the partner of a brain injured person and/or the injured person is also a parent. If you don't read it, even just working through the end-of-chapter exercises would be enormously helpful."
—BI FAMILY MEMBER LEE W., NEW ZEALAND

"Everyone who is touched by a brain injury should read this book."
—RETIRED DEFENSE AND VETERANS HEAD INJURY

PROGRAM MANAGER LYNETTE PERRY, NAVAL MEDICAL CENTER, CALIFORNIA

IN GRATITUDE

To the families who shared their stories

To the therapists who never give up

To my friends who stuck with me through the worst of it. Marty Traynor, Bonnie Pfeifer, Jan Jervis, Wanda Knauer.

And above all, for my family who did the best they could every day. Dale, Mike, Kara, Mom and brother Steve. I wouldn't have made it through the dark years without you.

Introduction

When I was a kid, and I fell down and skinned my knee or got a splinter under my fingernail, I would go to my father for help.

"It hurts," I would cry.

My father, who had seen many mishaps himself while growing up, would grin.

"That's good," he'd say. "Pain builds character."

Now that a member of your family has been brain injured, you're going to get a lot of chances to build your character. Because this hurts. And no matter what you do, it isn't going to stop hurting.

And this book won't stop the hurting either. It isn't going to make your decisions for you. It isn't going to soothe the pain you feel. But it may help you get through the toughest times by reminding you that thousands of other people, just like you and your family, have been through it too. And we've survived.

I wish there were easy answers to the problems you will face now that you have a brain-injured family member or friend, but there aren't any. And no matter how sure of themselves they seem, none of the experts have easy answers for you either.

It's up to you to pick your way through some extremely rocky paths. Sometimes you may think you can't go on, and many times you will wonder if anyone cares.

Yes. We do.

This book is not a substitute for good therapy from a professional. I believe that sometimes we get too overwhelmed to be able to view our own lives with any perspective at all, and at times like these we should seek out a trained counselor. Don't deny yourself their good work if you feel as though your life is out of control.

The people in this book have been very honest about their experiences, and to avoid any embarrassment they might feel, I have kept their identities to myself. The names used are fictitious except for those of my own family.

My family is typical of the families you will meet, and you will get to know us well. My husband Dale suffered brain damage during a life-saving operation, and my daughter, Kara, and son, Mike, had to deal with problems that are unknown to many of their schoolmates. We have traveled a journey of experiences that seemed unbelievable then, but now is just part of our lives. You will get a chance to laugh along with us about some of our most absurd experiences, and you may cry along with us at some of our most painful.

Some of the painful stories in this book need to be told because they are real and "normal" when we're dealing with brain injury. He doesn't remember much about the times he was unpredictable and sometimes violent. Those things were caused by the injury to his brain and the tremendous emotional pressure he was under, not because he was a bad person. Although he is not perfect and is not the same as he was before his injury, most of those problems have been dealt with.

Dale has made enormous progress both intellectually and emotionally. In many ways this injury has made him a better man. He is more sensitive and compassionate. It may seem to some readers as though we must be a miserable family, but we aren't. Even though Dale decided a divorce would free all of us from his problems, we are still a warm and loving family. The things that happened to us over a number of years have made us more aware of others who are in pain, and we have grown from the experiences. Our worst times were the first years after Dale's injury when our lives were undergoing immense changes. His temper is now mostly under control (something I had wished for in vain before his brain injury) and he is willing to listen to other points of view. I expected, in the beginning, that he would go back to alcohol to dull his terrible pain, but he has not. He has accepted the great burden of brain injury with more grace and patience than I ever would have expected from him.

I hope I have weathered this crisis as well as he has. When Dale was first injured, some of my friends advised me to get out of the marriage. I had my own life to think about, they told me. I should not burden myself and my children with this heavy load. But if I had walked away from him when he needed me, would my life have been a success? Perhaps. Perhaps not. I will never know if my family would have been better or worse off if I had made a different choice. I only knew that I had a decision to make. If you are faced with a situation that seems like abandonment, balance the good and the bad, choose, then don't look back. That is, after all, what coping is all about.

Every year in the United States, over 1.5 million people suffer brain injury. Millions of families deal with the consequences. Depression, role changes, grief and stress play havoc with what may have once been a normal, happy family. Financial pressures may mount to unbearable levels, threatening a family's future. Homes may be lost. College forgone. Retirement postponed. Siblings and spouses may become resentful and angry when their needs are put aside because of an injured family member.

Most of the doctors and other health professionals you meet will have your brain injured family member as their priority. Very few understand, unless they have actually lived with a brain injury victim, what you are going through. You may even help them stay unaware because you act as if you are managing bravely whenever you see them.

But I know what you're going through and the people you meet on the following pages understand how you're feeling. We hope that what we've learned will help you in your struggle to deal with brain injury in the family.

Courage, fellow traveler. You are not alone.

The Brain

I won't attempt to give you a detailed, clinical view of the brain. The first reason is that I don't know enough about it to be very precise, and there are many books you can read that will supply that technical information for you. And let's face it; you may have heard all you can stand to hear about the brain for right now.

But the brain is the reason you're reading this book, and it is a fascinating subject. When I first started trying to learn about the brain, I thought researchers must have all the answers. The explanations are so precise and authoritative. The answers all seem so obvious. Yet, the more I read and the more brain injured people I meet, the more I understand that modern medicine's understanding of the human brain is nowhere near enough. While we've learned a great deal about the brain, no matter how much we learn, we'll probably never know enough to make the severely injured brain whole again.

That's why, for months, the doctor can't tell you very much about your brain-injured family member. He can guess. He can speculate about recovery. But he really doesn't know what will happen. The brain does its own thing. Sometimes a person will make a miraculous recovery when all the experts said he would never reach a functional level. But many times he won't, even though all the signs pointed to full recovery. Nobody knows why.

I think being a neurologist or neurosurgeon must be the most frustrating job in the world—other than being the caregiver to a brain-injured person.

The brain is a truly remarkable organ. Everything we do is controlled there. Our dreams, our plans, our bad temper or our ability to make puns—they all exist inside our brains. It keeps our blood pumping, allows us to recognize Great Aunt Emma and encourages us to take three giant steps backward when we encounter a rattlesnake, even if we've never seen one before.

And it only weighs three pounds. My computer weighs more than that and it can certainly calculate faster than my brain—if we're talking about numbers. But my computer can't tell me when it's cold or dream about winning the lottery. There are billions of cells in my brain—only about a tenth of them active nerve cells—but those nerve cells have lots of contacts with other cells.

The brain has three parts. The forebrain is the part you probably see when you think about the brain. Formed primarily by the two cerebral hemispheres where most of the high functions of our intellect take place, the forebrain also includes smaller parts: the thalamus, hypothalamus, basal ganglia, olfactory lobes and optic nerves. The forebrain is where we think, make decisions, remember and perceive. The smaller nerve clusters are the coordinators and communicators of the brain, passing on information for the cerebrum to consider. The thalamus receives information from the body's senses and sends out commands to the muscles. The hypothalamus plays a crucial part in our emotions and controls our involuntary movements— breathing, vomiting, blood pressure. The basal ganglia help regulate body movements, the optic nerves regulate eyesight and the olfactory lobes tell you when dinner is burning.

The midbrain, technically the shortest, highest section of the brainstem, is the relay center for the body's senses. Below that is the hindbrain, including the pons and medulla, the two lowest sections of the brainstem. The hindbrain has links with special sensors, and the crisscrossing of the nerve fibers in the medulla allows for the cross-brain organization where the left side of the brain controls the right side of the body and the right controls the left.

The brain can be further divided by the fissures or "ditches" that run through the cerebrum. From front to back, the longitudinal sulcus separates the left of the cerebrum from the right. The two sides seem to mirror each other although they have quite different duties.

Another "ditch" called the central fissure runs from side to side from about the back of the ear across the top of the head to the back of the other ear. This fissure separates the frontal lobes of the brain from the parietal and occipital lobes. If we were traveling back from the central fissure, we would first enter the parietal lobe where sensory information is digested, and then the occipital lobe where the visual center is located. A person with an injury to the parietal lobe may be able to feel pain but not know where the pain is located, while an injury to the occipital lobe could leave a person blind.

In the temporal lobe, separated from the other lobes by the Sylvian fissure running from front to back above the ear, are housed the centers of hearing and memory as well as the senses of time and individuality. Because of the temporal lobe's connections with the hindbrain (our animal brain) we also experience fear, lust and anger here.

Even the mirror-image left and right sides of our brains have separate tasks. The left side of our brain seems to house our language and fine motor skills. However, if we write novels or paint beautiful landscapes, we are probably dominated by the right side of our brain. The right side of our brain seems to make symbolic language skills possible. However, if we are more likely to work a crossword puzzle or work as an accountant, our left side is probably dominant. Our left hemisphere remembers Aunt Bessie's face, but our right side remembers her name and the smell of those great chocolate cookies she makes. Our right side sees the snow drifted beside the house and compares it to cotton candy. Our left sees the same snow and gets out the snow shovel. Dale and I are good examples of the differences of those dominated by different sides of the brain. He is a left-dominant person. He was an engineer who worked with math and who did wood working as a hobby. I am a right-dominant person. I am a writer who works with words. He likes neatness, precision and straight lines. I like a little clutter, don't believe that anything is precise, and can't abide straight lines. He plans. I dream.

Although scientists first determined that the speech and writing skills were located in the left hemisphere, they now believe that the emotion aspects of speech and writing are located in the right. The brain, in order to operate in what we perceive is a normal fashion, must use both sides of the brain. Of course the separations between the brain areas and brain tasks are incomplete. The tasks carried out by one part of the brain are affected by other parts of the brain so that no one lobe or hemisphere works well without the others. In a relatively minor injury, other brain cells may take over the job of the cells that were damaged and the brain will continue to hum along with only a small tic. However, a major injury to any of these areas can seriously interrupt the brain's operation. As a car traveling with one flat tire jostles its riders and destroys some of the machinery, the brain will not operate smoothly without all the pieces working together.

So if some healthy brain cells can take over for damaged brain cells, isn't it possible that all but the most serious brain injury can be overcome? Maybe or maybe not. It depends on which expert you talk to. Certainly if most of the temporal lobe is destroyed, there is little chance that there will be enough left to retrain. But some researchers believe that with enough diligence, research and new scientific breakthroughs, people can achieve remarkable recoveries. The younger a person is when an injury occurs, the more fully that person is likely to recover. New therapy techniques are bringing stroke victims back to a functional level where 20 years ago they would have been put in a rest home to vegetate.

I'm an optimist. I believe the possibilities are enormous for a brain-injured person to make significant recovery. I've seen too many people who were told by the experts that they would never be able to walk or speak or reason again who are doing just those things. They may not be perfect, but they are huge jumps beyond where they were when they were told to give up.

Therapists tend not to be very supportive of such a contention. They work with people who struggle for years and never achieve their goals. They see the emotional turmoil of such a struggle and often contend that it's better to accept early on that recovery isn't possible. I am sure that theory is correct in some cases and incorrect in others.

But the brain is a remarkable organ that we don't fully understand. Who knows what the possibilities may be? Research continues and new ideas come along every day. The jury is still out on recovery from brain injury.

Shattered Dreams

Dale and I were the stereotypical high school sweethearts. We met at the local college hangout where he worked the counter and where I could count on an extra-large serving of french fries. He was smart and ambitious and always setting goals, meeting them, and then setting more. We went steady in high school, were engaged while he was serving on an aircraft carrier off the shores of Viet Nam. We were married when I was 19 and he was 20. With the help of his GI Bill benefits, he went to engineering school while I worked. After graduation Dale was hired as an engineer for Eastman Kodak and we began our family with Mike. Kara followed two years later. I went back for my college degree after the kids were in school. Things were going well for us. Dale was a successful engineer and I was a newspaper editor. The kids were active in sports and doing well in school. We had dreams of fixing up the house, of seeing the kids graduate from college and establishing their own successful lives. In short, we were a pretty normal family.

He was only 38 when the doctors first discovered the aneurysm in Dale's brain, almost by accident. He complained of difficulty reading. He went to an ophthalmologist for an eye exam and was told that stress was tiring his eyes and he should rest more. So he rested, but it didn't help. The second ophthalmologist gave Dale several tests, one of which showed blind spots which might be caused by pressure somewhere in his brain. Then came the neurologist and the CT scan that showed the golf ball-size aneurysm in the center of his brain.

The choices were few. It basically boiled down to a choice of do something or do nothing. The latter choice meant probable death or certain massive brain damage should the aneurysm burst. The neurologist gave us the other choice: brain surgery. It might cause brain damage too, but at least there would be a chance of success and a good chance of saving Dale's life.

So I sent a warm, intelligent, articulate man off to surgery and received a confused, irrational, childlike man in return. He could not speak or understand me. He could not walk, or reason or remember where his elbow was. I could not believe that this had happened to us and I did not believe that it was permanent. And, although it seemed at the time to be a rational choice, I didn't do what I really wanted to do—run screaming from that hospital room.

Before we came to know brain injury, most of us probably took our brains pretty much for granted. Oh, we might have thought of ourselves as bright or not-so-bright. We could even joke about killing off our brain cells while we participated in an attitude adjustment session at the neighborhood bar. But I would venture a guess that few of us ever worried about brain injury the way we might have worried about heart attack or AIDS or cancer.

So when someone we love is brain injured, we know next to nothing about brain functions or about the much larger issue of what brain damage means to us. I had been exposed to some anatomy in my science classes in high school and college. My brother is a veterinary neurologist and my mother was a medical technologist. I had as much exposure as most people outside the medical field, and yet I was ignorant of even the most basic brain functions. It's not surprising. Surviving serious brain injury is a relatively new phenomenon.

There is much philosophical discussion within the medical profession over the brain-mind division. Some researchers contend that the brain is different than the mind. The mind is a blend of spirituality and chemical function, they believe, while the brain is just another organ. (Please forgive my simplistic explanation. All the explanations in this book are simplified and delivered through the filter of lay experience with brain injury. If you are interested in a more technical explanation, there are thousands of resources on the internet.)

Such philosophy is no doubt valuable, but for me and for others in my situation, it has little practical meaning. My brain-injured husband is not the same person he was before. In some ways he is a better person, but he is not the same. After years of experience with brain injury, I am sure there is rarely, if ever, 100 percent recovery from any serious brain injury. That is not to say that a survivor is not lovable and valued by his or her family, but he is no longer the same person. He can be a functioning member of the family, but he may function in a different manner.

Suppose you have spent weeks putting together a jigsaw puzzle on the living room table. The puzzle is a gift from your friend Mary, and the picture is a portrait of her. On the wall nearby is a black-and-white portrait of her taken when you were in college. Mary is beautiful isn't she?

But as the puzzle comes together it's apparent that at the factory, a couple of pieces must have been dropped. The puzzle is incomplete and the pieces must have gotten mixed with pieces of other puzzles. Mary's hair is splotchy red and black, and isn't that a five o'clock shadow on the left side of her chin? Oh my goodness, one eyebrow is bushy and streaked with grey while the other is black and neatly plucked. You stare at this portrait with disbelief. It is certainly not the same as the portrait on the wall. True, it's an interesting puzzle, but it's not Mary's image. You tear the puzzle apart and throw the pieces back in the box. This isn't right. The puzzle must go back to the factory and the factory must send you one that looks right.

But while you're packing up the puzzle the doorbell rings and you open the door to find Mary standing on your doorstep. It doesn't take but a moment to realize that the person standing in the doorway looks exactly like the puzzle portrait. In the five years since you've seen Mary, she's changed! The picture on the wall is the before picture. Mary is standing before you, her hair mottled red and black, one bushy grey eyebrow and a patch of whiskers on her chin. No way! There's been a mistake. Bring back the real Mary. You loved her for her silky red hair and lovely face. THIS isn't the Mary you loved!

So it goes with a brain injury. From the very first day your family member is injured, reality becomes incomprehensible. How could this person you love be so different? No way, you protest. There's been a mistake. Bring back the original.

Just as the loss of a few pieces of a beautiful jigsaw puzzle distorts the picture, head injury, with its missing pieces of personality, distorts our perception of that person we love. The brain is the very basis of personality, and yet it operates in such delicate balance that we pay attention to it only when it malfunctions or is injured. We breathe, we argue, we judge, we run, we weep or laugh all because our brain is merrily chugging away at a communication job that makes the calculations of the most sophisticated computer seem as simple as counting on fingers and toes. The brain most certainly determines the person. It controls our physical actions, and it is the base of all our emotions and thoughts.

A person with an injury to his brain loses control of his emotional being. These significant changes may be a loss of the ability to feel emotion or total lack of control over those emotions. Those are incredible changes for us, as family members, to accept and to cope with.

If your father has always been a gentle, easy-going, loving man, you will have a great deal of difficulty associating those memories with the man who, after a stroke, is morose, angry and threatening. If your daughter was a sweet, affectionate, joyful little girl before she was injured, you may not recognize the child who cannot respond to any affection and who seems uninterested in the rest of the world.

The college professor who can no longer read or speak, the accountant who can no longer add two and two, the athlete who struggles to feed himself—they are not the same people they were before. Yes, sometimes they seem the same. Maybe for an instant you see that same smile, feel that same gentle touch, hear the familiar silly giggle.

Family members, in particular, bear the brunt of the change. We feel a deep commitment to help. But most often, we want to help in a way that will bring back the person who was there before—something that may not be possible.

Therein lies the dilemma with which family members continually attempt to cope. It's the catch-22 of modern medicine. Yes, they saved my child's life, but they didn't bring back the same child. Yes, my husband's survival is miraculous, but the life we had before is over.

What an unbelievable piece of information that has been to accept. I'm married to a man I might not have considered loving before. It's as if I woke up one morning and found a stranger in my bed—a stranger whose needs are enormous.

But that's not all. Imagine this! Everyone else thinks that he's the same. "Oh yes," they say, "he's been sick so you have to make allowances, but he's just the same. Just look at him. He's the same man you promised to stick with in sickness and health, so you'd better just get used to it. You're his family. It's your duty."

And no one preached that sentiment louder than I said it to myself.

But we were all wrong about one thing.

He's not the same man.

I need no further proof that the brain is indeed the mind.

First Fears

I'm sure Dale's surgeon would not have approved of the way we first heard that Dale had suffered a brain injury. My brother, my mother, Dale's mom and I were gathered in the family area of the hospital, where the diagnostic and x-ray services were done, along with kids with sprained ankles, pregnant women waiting for an ultrasound test, and old men suffering from barium indigestion. The procedure Dale was undergoing was delicate and needed constant surveillance. The hours dragged by. Other patients had come and gone. The surgeon had estimated two to three hours for the procedure and had come into the room after four hours to tell us that things were going all right, just slowly. After six hours, the radiologist hurried out of the room, pausing to tell us, "We had a few little problems. The doc will be out in a minute to explain."

By the time the surgeon entered the room 15 minutes later, we had little patience for the technical details. "Don't tell me about spasms and aphasia," I wanted to shout at him. "How bad is it?"

Later, I stood beside my husband's hospital bed and watched his eyes wander around the room. They hesitated for a moment on my face and then wandered away without showing any recognition. When I talked to him he would struggle to focus, but it wouldn't last more than an instant.

The next day, after a sleepless night, I entered the intensive care room to find Dale sitting in a chair beside his bed. Mary, the ICU nurse, expressed pleasure to see me and suggested that since it was time for lunch, I sit with Dale and help him eat. She tried to prepare me. "He's still a little confused but try to let him do everything for himself," she said. It sounded like such silly advice—when had Dale not done anything he wanted for himself? Mary set the lunch tray on the table in front of him, placed a spoon in his hand and went away.

Dale's eyes wandered around the room for a few moments. His head drooped occasionally and then cocked at a strange angle. He studied the spoon in his hand for what seemed like hours, and then he carefully put it to his mouth and began to suck on it. He did not know what the spoon was for or how to use it.

I was devastated. I just sat there staring at him. Mary came back, took his hand and showed him how to use the spoon. "He just needs a little reminder," she said. She must have known how shocked I was, though I tried hard to show that I wasn't affected by the strangeness I was seeing. She had probably seen it many times before.

Yet, despite my calm smiles and apparently easy conversation with both Mary and Dale, I could hardly breathe. As a newspaper reporter and editor, I had taught myself not to show by my appearance what I was thinking. If during an interview I let my shock or anger show, I would not get the information I wanted. It is a useful tool, and I found myself using it a lot over the first few months after Dale's surgery. Because that day in the hospital, for the first time, I really began to fear the future.

Dale's father was much more straightforward in his reaction. After his first visit to the intensive care unit, tears flowed down his face as he looked at me. "He doesn't recognize me. He can't talk—he just babbles like a baby. He can't even squeeze my hand. He can't focus his eyes." His head dropped to his hands as he wept. "He's just a vegetable."

No one is prepared for the profound changes that occur between the healthy family member of "before" and the one lying in the hospital with a brain injury. Those changes are frightening beyond description to a family. We are used to frightening possibilities with heart surgery, but although that heart patient is very ill and may die, he or she is still the same person. He can smile when he sees you, or speak your name, or reach out to touch you.

But a brain injury is often very different. Like a bomb that goes off in the command center of a computerized factory, a brain injury damages the complex system of controls which keeps things running in a familiar pattern. Fuses are blown and the communication system shorts out.

And that's pretty frightening. Particularly since that person has suddenly become a stranger. Since the essence of our personalities lies in our brains somewhere, when the brain of our family member is damaged and starts sending out confused messages, we don't recognize that person anymore.

So Dale's father wept and compared him to a vegetable. I sat on the hard vinyl chairs and refused to believe anything that had happened would last. I read magazines as if to prove that everything was normal. I could not face what might be coming, so I pretended this terrible thing was going to go away if I remained calm and in control. Things would get back on schedule in a few weeks—a few months at most.

That wasn't to be. Nothing will ever be the same again for our family—not the schedule, not the people, not the life we lived. If we are lucky, it will be nearly the same. But no one goes through a brain injury without being changed in some way. If Dale recovers completely, he will nevertheless have struggled with a difficult task to do so.

But like most brain-injured people, Dale probably will not recover all that he has lost. He will live without some things he had before. It may be a portion of his memory. It may be his articulate way of expressing himself. It may be the grace and athletic ability, or the clear-eyed logic that once made him sought after by his associates. Sometimes I think Dale has lost the very things that made me fall in love with him.

One thing that families of a brain-injured individual must develop if they are to cope is patience. The brain does not heal quickly. This injury is not like a broken leg which can be cast, keeps you out of circulation for a few weeks, and then heals as good as new. The brain is so complex that specialists don't totally understand it, much less understand how to fix it. So it's up to the brain to heal itself. Sometimes it can't and sometimes it can. But the only way to find out is to give it a chance, and that takes time.

So spend your time learning. Try to forget the "how bad is it?" questions and start learning about the brain. Find out what brain functions this injury will affect and how to help overcome the problems that might occur. Read about theories, particularly those that disagree with each other, concerning how the brain relearns its functions. Talk to specialists. Read about people who've recovered and those who did not but were able to make their lives meaningful. Do something positive.

The knowledge you acquire from this research will help you to overcome the fear you're feeling. It will give you information that will help you understand your physician's and therapist's instructions and reasoning. It will become your first step back toward control over your life.

And spend some of your time grieving. Grieve for what you have lost. Get angry. Throw things. Cry. You have the right to be angry. You have the right to feel cheated.

Some plans are going to have to be made. But before you can begin the plans, you must first accept that you are planning a life that is different—altogether more challenging but not necessarily worse—than the one you had planned before.

So have a good cry. Punch the wall. Kick the furniture. Then take a deep breath, stick out your chin and get on with it.

It will hurt, but you're stronger than you think you are. You can take it.

EXERCISE

Your physician can't tell you what the eventual outcome of this brain injury will be because each brain injury reacts differently. And because that's all you can think about, you tend to forget to ask pertinent questions and remember the answer to questions you do remember to ask. Focusing on what is happening right now, and your own response to it, may help you stay on track. The exercise below may help you work through this initial period.

1. Invest in a notebook that you can carry with you in your purse, briefcase, or under your arm. You'll be writing quite a lot and will be glad you have this notebook. Carry it with you every time you see the doctor or anyone else involved in your family member's care. Write a list of all the questions to which you want answers concerning your family member's brain injury, OTHER THAN what the eventual outcome will be. (For example: What physical functions might this injury affect? Or, why does your family member fly into temper tantrums and how can you avoid that?)

2. The next time you visit with your physician, ask him or her the questions listed in the first part of this exercise and WRITE DOWN THE ANSWERS UNDER THE QUESTION IN YOUR NOTEBOOK. This way you will have a permanent record of them and be able to go back and refer to this information if you forget.

3. Think about your experiences with brain injury so far and list five fears that you are experiencing. Have each member of the family do the same, if possible. Discuss the fears and how you can create strategies to alleviate them. (REMEMBER: Each person's fear is very personal and most important to him or her. Every fear is a reasonable one, at least until a strategy is created which alleviates it.)

The Power of Anger

Anger is a powerful change agent.

I was angry with my father-in-law when he called my husband a vegetable. Part of that anger was a healthy case of denial and part of it was the knowledge that the doctor was very hopeful about recovery. But, as I watched Dale struggling to feed himself, it finally became apparent to me that this was going to go on for a long time. It wasn't going to clear up in a few months. In a sense, I was on my own. I must assume responsibility for all those things that I had formerly only dealt with as a team member. I would have to make the decisions about how to spend our dwindling money—alone. I would have to take responsibility for the children—alone. And I would have to take responsibility for a man who did not know how to feed himself. I was totally overwhelmed and had never felt lonelier in my life.

For a while, I let myself be steered by social workers and therapists and Dale's doctor. I was more compliant than I had ever been in my life. It was all I could do to figure out which fast food place I should take the kids to for dinner, let alone actually make dinner. How could I make decisions about therapy? I let the professionals make my decisions for me because they supposedly knew best. Of course, everyone around me had advice. People made suggestions and I attempted to listen, usually mumbling something like, "That's probably a good idea," or "I'll have to check on that." But I was no more capable of handling any decisions about our future than was my 12-year-old daughter.

It all came to a head when Mother's Day, my birthday and my daughter's birthday came all in the same week. Actually my birthday and Mother's Day were the same day. And no one remembered—not even me for a few hours. Dale had come home from the hospital only a few days before. I was trying to run a newspaper, get him to therapy twice a day, keep the children's lives on an even keel, and check on Dale's activities at lunchtime each day. I was exhausted. I talked to my mother; we wished each other a happy Mother's Day. My kids said happy Mother's Day and apologized for not having a present for me but there had been no one to take them to town or give them the money to do so. I hugged them and acted as if it didn't matter, but it did. And that night I cried myself to sleep.

Two days later, I realized it was my daughter's birthday and I hadn't had time to get her a present. I bought a birthday cake at the store, remembering my own bad birthday and now realizing that I was a terrible mother with no present to give my daughter. I hurried home with the cake and, as I tried to explain about not having time to buy her a present, I began to cry. For the first time in months, I let myself go in front of the kids. My daughter hugged me and told me it didn't matter just as I had done for her only days before. And, of course, I knew that it mattered to her even more than my similar experience had mattered to me. We were a mess! And I was mad about it.

Such blossoms of anger took a while to turn into a full-fledge, blood-red flower of rage. I had passed through the first stages of shock, disbelief and denial and the anger was growing every day. One of the first buds appeared briefly, just for a moment, when I met the hospital social worker when Dale was discharged. Her first words to Dale (while looking directly at me) were, "Your doctor says you should recover completely—and you might."

Those words said two things to me. First I heard, "your doctor is lying to you." The second thing I heard was that Dale had very little chance of recovering.

How dare she say that? How dare she heap more doubt and pain on my shoulders, I thought. But my denial process was working well at that point, and I shrugged it off. I consoled myself by thinking she just had no idea about the facts. She didn't know that MY husband was ACTUALLY going to recover. This case would be different than most, and she just didn't realize that. After all, we didn't even need her advice because in a few months everything would be back to normal.

It took the birthday chaos to bring all the little bits of anger up that I'd been hiding from myself. I had been taught all my life that a positive attitude was the only way in which to approach life. My parents taught me that I could do anything I wanted if I approached it with the right attitude and worked hard enough at it. My grandfather, a successful rancher and land developer, who had died only a few years before, had often repeated a simple phrase which I had etched indelibly in my mind: "Never ever lose your temper until you're absolutely sure you've lost."

Well, I had lost. Those family words of wisdom might have worked well for me before, but maintaining control of my attitude and our lives had become an impossible burden. No matter how positive I was, things were still awful! People admired my ability to deal with my crisis and continue my demanding lifestyle at the newspaper. They told me how amazing I was. They couldn't see through the calm exterior to realize that I was on the verge of collapse, emotionally and physically. A lot of people asked what they could do to help but few actually made any effort. And to ask for help somehow seemed like failure to me.

And I was angry because I didn't think I should have to fail at this. In the beginning my anger was mostly self-directed. Somehow, I felt that I should have been able to handle this crisis better than I was doing—as well as people kept telling me I was doing. I was an intelligent, capable woman. Yet here I was, letting others tell me what to do and not even being able to keep things running smoothly for my children. I constantly berated myself for being so incompetent and weak. I let the bills pile up on the desk. I hadn't responded to any of the questionnaires and forms that the hospital and insurance companies required. My kids were having to do their own laundry, to remind me to make appointments, things I'd always done for them before. I felt I was neglecting them. I had even forgotten to call their schools to explain why they weren't getting homework done and seemed so frantic. I felt guilty and like a failure.

But then I began to blame others. I was angry that people couldn't see that I was in trouble, even though I was doing my best to keep them from knowing it. I was angry that this had happened to my family—we'd worked hard and were good people. None of our mistakes deserved this kind of punishment. I was angry with Dale for causing me so much pain. I didn't care that he had no control over what had happened. I was just mad at him because he had made my life difficult even though I had been a good wife. There had been years of dealing with a drinking problem, and I had stuck with him through that. I had been trying hard to make the transition from my being a homemaker to being a working woman easier for him. How could he have heaped this problem on me too? I was angry at myself for even getting married to him. I was really angry at people who kept telling me that this crisis would bring my family closer and would make us stronger. I was angry at the insurance companies and Dale's company for not giving me information I needed to have without my having to harass them.

It took my friends to make me understand that my kids were old enough to be taking on responsibilities. "Look," they said, "we thought you were a liberated woman. Don't you want your kids to be capable of taking care of themselves? Didn't you know how to do those things when you were their age?" And so I began to see my children in a different light—not as infants who needed my protection but as young people who needed to assume their places in the world. And most of all, my friends told me, Mike and Kara needed to be able to have some control over their own lives. If they were doing their own laundry, they would be sure that it got done. They were also intelligent and capable and, with the increased responsibilities and stresses the family had to cope with, they felt that they were helping out when they took on those responsibilities. I had forgotten that the whole family was included in this crisis, not just me.

And the anger began to mobilize me. I began to be more assertive—to tell people what I thought about their system of health care, about the way they treated people. I began to try to make sense out of our lives again. As I grew more angry and determined to get things under my own control again, the fear began to lapse just a little. But as much as I'd like to say it's gone, it still comes back when things are difficult.

But with the anger, something else came as well—a certain acceptance and a resolve to make the best of a bad situation. I cannot say that I accepted that Dale's brain injury would be permanent. But I did accept that things were going to be different for a long time. I began to accept that I didn't have to fail. And at the time I was struggling with that new idea, I was slowly turning my anger away from myself and going on to grieve what we had lost.

Getting Through the Grief

For at least three years after Dale's surgery, our life seemed as though we were trapped in the house of mirrors at a carnival. No matter which way I turned, I was greeted with a new image, a new perception. There were days when I would tell Dale's parents that I thought he was going to recover completely and then 15 minutes later, I would tell my mother that he would never get any better. Some days I was filled with hope as Dale accomplished something new, only to be plunged into depression when he would erupt into a rage of frustration over some small misunderstanding.

There is no adequate way to describe the force of grief. It became an overwhelming, dominating force in our lives when Dale's brain was injured. I expected to feel badly about the tragedy that had befallen my husband, but I didn't expect the upheaval and confusion in my most basic beliefs and in my relationships with family and friends. I didn't expect that my children would suffer so much and I didn't expect our lives to turn into such a nightmare.

I had read a little about the grief process when my father died. The first stage is shock, quickly followed by denial. The denial state, in death, is often put to an end by a funeral or the giving away of that person's belongs. Other emotions last longer—guilt, anger and depression. And according to the experts on grief, when we work through all those emotions we can finally arrive at acceptance—a stage where we can get on with our lives.

I did struggle with my father's death for what seemed then like a very long time, and I can identify times when I went through all those stages. Although I still miss him after all these years, the grief process that I went through after his death is very different from what we've been through since Dale was brain-injured.

When my father died, he left us irrevocably. I had no false hopes that he would return. I had only to deal with my own loss and to accept that emptiness in my life.

But when Dale was injured, my grief was less coherent, more chaotic, more long-lasting than the grief that followed my father's death. Dale didn't leave us—exactly. But I couldn't identify how much of him we had lost or how much would come back. Every loss was subjective and very likely to change. Our lives were suddenly very different, but before I could identify how much different, everything would change. I didn't know what I was supposed to deny. Who should I be angry with? Do I feel guilty because I've done something wrong or because I feel sorry for him? Exactly what should I accept so I can get on with my life? Nothing stays the same long enough for me to get used to it. Except, of course, for the pain.

The stages of grief are supposed to have ends and beginnings. But with Dale's brain injury, the stages have had no edges at all. On any given day I still may pass through denial, anger and acceptance and end up going to bed tied up in guilt. Depression is a constant companion. I can identify what I'm feeling, and I can even get through to acceptance.

And then something changes. Dale experiences a breakthrough that sends him broadjumping past his earlier limitations. Or we receive a notice in the mail that our disability payment may be canceled.

ZAP! I'm back on the treadmill again. I may be involved in the normal process of grief. But I FEEL like I'm going crazy. Again and again.

Shock simplified my life for a couple of days after Dale's surgery. I simply refused to accept any information about brain damage. Oh sure, I listened politely to the doctor, and I asked all the right questions. But nothing was actually computing. My philosophy was to ignore it and it would go away. I wasn't feeling anything at all. Even though I probably hadn't slept more than three hours a night for a couple of weeks, I was cheerful and diligent at work. I was relatively patient with the kids, and we went out for hamburgers and pizza. Dale might just as well have been away on a business trip.

I stumbled into denial when I watched him suck on that spoon because he didn't know what it was for. And I grabbed on to it wholeheartedly when the social worker straightforwardly said that recover wasn't necessarily a sure thing. Okay, I could accept that he had a problem. But it wouldn't last.

Denial has a life of its own, and its longevity is remarkable. Denial is good and bad. It can hurt and it can heal. And when we're dealing with brain injury, it is an absolutely necessary tool for family members. Without it, we could not get out of bed in the morning. We could not choose medical facilities or pay our doctor bills or deal with any of our problems in a rational manner. If we accepted the enormity of our problems immediately, we could not function.

Someone once asked me how I dealt with all the details of brain injury—how I coped with the children's problems, the problems at work, financial problems and Dale's injury. It's very simple, I told them. I don't. I put things on a mental shelf until they absolutely cannot be ignored any longer. I deal with only as much as I can endure at one time.

Health professionals sometimes seem inordinately concerned about denial and unrealistic expectations of family members and of the brain-injured themselves. I believe this comes from their having to watch people struggle to overcome their limitations without gain. But I believe that the insistence of therapists and other professionals that we must give up denial and learn to accept "the facts" is a well-intentioned mistake. Although denial makes moving on to a more peaceful emotional state very difficult, it is nevertheless what turns the impossible into the possible.

One mother was firmly entrenched in denial. She refused to accept that her son didn't recognize or couldn't respond. The doctor told her he was deaf. She refused to believe that too. They told her he would have to be institutionalized, probably for life. She denied that. She refused to listen to the well-intentioned efforts by relatives and friends to get her to put the boy in and institution where he would be cared for. She created all kinds of problems for herself, her doctor, the hospital staff and her family.

But she was right. He did hear her and after a time, could respond. He did learn to walk, to feed himself and to get around. He was not the hopeless case her relatives had told her to forget. If she had listened to all the medical opinions that she received, she would have given up, and the boy would still be in an institution, no doubt nowhere near as functional as he is now. The boy's quality of life would have been dismal compared to what he has now.

But it hasn't been easy. The family has struggled. Each member bears scars from this ordeal. They have lost friends and grown distant from their relatives. The have fired doctors, nurses and therapists who did not share their belief and commitment to their son, making a name for themselves in the medical community as troublemakers. The parents have considered divorce, and the house is still full of tension after many years. There is pain in abundance.

Were the sacrifices worth the rewards? They believe so. Had they been able to feel that their emotions were normal and been able to talk to each other, their struggle might have left fewer scars. They can look back now and see many of their own mistakes, but seeing that mistakes were made does not lessen the pain. Yet, they don't use the word denial except in reference to what a therapist might have said to them. They talk about hope.

There is the dilemma of denial. Denial and hope are the same shoe in different colors. Denial can cause us to drive our brain injured family member too hard while hope may help us demand enough to bring recovery. Denial can cause psychological damage, while hope may keep us sane.

Can we accept that our family member is brain damaged and hope for a full recovery at the same time? Yes we can. Most family members sit on this seesaw continually, and the weathered old board is full of splinters. Finding a comfortable spot is next to impossible.

People who deal with brain injury must find a way to expect enough without expecting too much. It makes a high wire act look like child's play. But as you struggle to balance hope and denial, remember that most of the world's real progress has been made by unreasonable people—people who would not listen to the facts.

Guilt

Oh how guilt can haunt you.

The night before his surgery, Dale jokingly told his mother that the aneurysm was her fault because the tendency ran in families. That joke haunted his mother for a very long time after he was disabled even though there was no way she could be blamed.

Guilt attacks you at the dinner table, wakes you in the night, and keeps you from enjoying the simple pleasures of life. It can drive you crazy, make you want to die, give you cancer, produce alcoholism and drug abuse.

A brain injury in the family will make guilt a constant companion. A disagreeable, hateful, unwelcome, persistent companion. If you have somehow indirectly or directly contributed to the brain injury, guilt will threaten to destroy your very soul. If you had nothing whatever to do with the injury, you may still feel guilty because you aren't doing enough, aren't being strong enough, are thinking bad thoughts—or even because you're healthy.

I sometimes feel guilty just going to the grocery store by myself because Dale isn't able to just get in the car and go wherever he wants. I feel guilty wanting to be by myself because he is often so isolated from friends.

Recently we attended a formal orchestra concert in which Mike was performing. The performers had been selected from schools throughout the state by audition, and Mike was one of six who had been selected from his high school. We were very proud of him as we sat in the crowded concert hall where the atmosphere was heavy with culture. The first piece played was a rousing number with an exciting melody, and there was a lot of foot tapping going on in the audience. Suddenly, Dale began to whistle along with the melody. Although my hand immediately closed on his knee like a vise, (my subtle way of telling him he was not behaving appropriately) many faces around us turned to stare. Since he had not realized that he was whistling along with the orchestra, Dale was embarrassed too. He rubbed knee where I had squeezed it and apologized. The look on his face made me feel very guilty and mean.

Oh dear, I had hurt him out of a fear of being embarrassed. How small and petty could I be? I quickly added that guilt to the enormous mound I carry around with me. In that mound is the guilt I feel for occasionally hating this new version of him. There's the guilt I feel for not being more understanding or more helpful or more demanding in his therapy. There's also plenty of guilt about the way I've handled the kids' problems and some guilt about wanting time for myself. And the guilt I carry with me is only the tip of the iceberg compared to the mountain of guilt that I keep on reserve.

Guilt eats at you because you have normal feelings and don't recognize that those feelings are at all legitimate. Like the father who wanted his son to die rather than to be "a vegetable," we all think thoughts that seem so terrible that we conclude we must be terrible people.

Even if we convince ourselves that the thoughts and the feelings are legitimate, few of us can get rid of the guilt. Normalcy is of very little comfort to most families of brain injury survivors. We already feel guilty for being normal—for walking and talking when our injured family member can't. I sometimes feel guilty for taking time out to read a book because Dale can't read. It doesn't seem fair that I should be able to. On other days I enjoy reading so much as an escape from dealing with Dale's problems that I feel guilty for enjoying it.

People tend to reinforce the guilt you're feeling. They don't mean to. They just don't understand the crazy things that are going on in your household, and they don't understand brain injury. So that makes it easy for them to criticize.

It happened for a purpose, they'll say. Or it happened because of something you did or didn't do. You're neglecting the brain-injured person and pampering the rest of the family. Or you're neglecting the rest of the family and pampering the one with the injury too much. You're wasting money on therapy, or you're too cheap to pay for therapy. You're not handling things the way you used to.

Of course, you're already saying those same things to yourself. I did. Actually, I still do. But I have to fight the guilt almost daily by telling myself I'm doing the best I can.

Dale and I have had an ongoing battle over the last 20 years about the different ways we approach life. I think it's worth some praise if someone does almost everything right in a project. Anybody who makes only one or two small mistakes deserves a pat on the back.

Dale reserves his praise for those who make no mistakes. There is no room for approval as long as there is a mistake in the final product.

You might see how that makes his recovery difficult. If I had to face my life with the attitude that one mistake is fatal, I would have been committed to the nearest asylum by now.

Even those people who do have some understanding and who are supportive of you can add to your guilt without meaning to.

My brother Steve has been wonderfully supportive. I know I can call him when Dale has gotten into an impossible thought pattern and is being so unreasonable that it threatens the family in some way. Dale will listen to Steve when nothing I say means anything to him.

Because he has a good working knowledge of the brain, my brother has also made many good suggestions about therapy. He's wonderful. He never criticizes, and he's helped me stay sane.

And because he's so supportive, I can experience enormous guilt pangs when we talk together. He's so darn reasonable. Here's an example.

Me: Boy, Dale has been impossible this week. He's got it into his head to reorganize the kitchen, and I can't find anything.

Steve: That's probably good for him. He probably realizes his organizational skills aren't good, and he's trying to relearn that skill.

Me: You're right. But I'm going crazy! I can't find anything in the kitchen, and he stands over my shoulder while I cook and makes me put everything back where I found it. (Knowing MY organizational skills, Steve laughs.)

Steve: It won't hurt you to get a little organized. It'll probably make things simpler for you.

Me: Yeah? Well I don't like it.

Steve: I don't blame you. I wouldn't like being forced into change either. But hang in there. As soon as he finishes this, he'll move on to another challenge.

Now how can you fault anyone for this kind of exchange? Steve was supportive of both of us. He pointed out the obvious good points while offering understanding for my discomfort.

But I still felt guilty after we talked. Why? Because he made it seem so obvious to me that I was being mean and demanding. I couldn't see that this simple problem of reorganization in the kitchen wasn't important in the larger scheme of Dale's recovering brain. I convinced myself that I was being selfish in wanting the kitchen to stay the same. Here I was complaining about him making progress.

Good grief. What a waste of energy. The guilt came from inside me, not from anything my brother said to me. He didn't say I was a selfish jerk, I did. I turned a very supportive conversation into guilt.

If we can feel so guilty about this kind of exchange, imagine the guilt we can feel if someone openly criticizes what we're doing for our brain-injured family member. It is very easy to turn to alcohol or drugs or food to dull the pain. Sometimes we bury ourselves in work or in a hobby in an effort to escape from the terrible burden of guilt that we feel.

The problem with all this guilt is that it makes us unable to function well in our families. It destroys our self-esteem, makes us wary and resentful.

Yes, we've all made mistakes. It's part of being human. Sometimes we've made grievous errors that have resulted in terrible pain to someone else. But if the guilt we feel about our mistakes overwhelms us, we won't be able to offer any support to our injured family member or to other family members who need us.

Our most important task is to forgive ourselves so that we can get on with life. If we can do that, we can forgive other people as well. Even the ones who criticize us out of ignorance.

Guilt doesn't change anything. It just makes us miserable—sometimes to the point of our becoming useless or even dangerous to our families. Yet we all experience it in varying degrees, from nearly overwhelming to overwhelming. Getting past it is difficult but necessary. If you can approach life as a project in which getting almost everything right is a victory instead of where making a mistake is a failure, you can manage the guilt. (Notice I didn't say get rid of it because I don't think any of us will be able to completely rid ourselves of guilt. But we can control it.)

It's even more necessary to control guilt than to balance denial and hope. Guilt will take away your humanity if you allow it. It will scar your relationship not only with the injured member of your family, but also with all of your family members. If you can't forgive yourself, guilt will make your life unbearable.

It will take a lot of internal dialogue to get through the times when you are truly convinced that you are a terrible person. Guilt is tenacious. It thrives on all our perceived inadequacies and our memories of past failures.

Sometimes our guilt is much too deep and overwhelming to talk about. We bury it inside where it eats away at our soul. If this is the way you feel, your minister, a therapist or counselor may be able to help you find peace.

You need to give yourself a break. You aren't perfect. All you can expect is the best you are able to do. That's all I can do. Would you expect more from me?

This is where detachment can be a useful tool. Only with guilt, you need to carry that detachment a step farther.

The code words are these: "I'm doing the best I can."

Terrible thoughts and wishes will continue to spring up in your mind. From wishing your child had died to being angry because your husband rearranges the kitchen—those resentments and wishes are normal. They are only reasonable responses to a life that has been drastically altered.

Do the best you can until you can do something different.

EXERCISE:

Guilt is one of the most destructive emotions that accompanies a head injury in the family. Each family member may be dealing with a different guilt feeling—guilt about disloyalty, guilt about actions which might have led to the brain injury, guilt about surviving, guilt about not liking the brain injured person. To help you identify what kinds of guilt you may be facing in your own personal situation, complete the exercise below. In your notebook make two columns. In the first column, list things that you know you feel guilty about. Then in the second column, list what you think is causing the guilt.

Guilt is a good teacher, but it is too often used as a punishment for something that can't be changed. To further expand your understanding of how to cope more successfully with guilt, take a moment to write your answers to the questions below:

1. What have I learned from this guilt.

2. How can what I've learned change the reality I face today?

3. How does my feeling guilty and miserable solve any of the problems I'm facing?

 4. Can I use this guilt in a more positive way? (Example: My driving drunk caused the accident. Now I'm teaching others about the perils of drunk driving.)

5   How is my guilt punishing other members of my family as well as myself?

EXERCISE

Take a moment to consider your answers to those questions.
Now ask if guilt is a useful factor in your life. If your answer is
no, read the list of possibilities below and consider the ideas that
you believe can be useful in helping you to handle guilt better.

_____ I am now ready to acknowledge that I am not personally
responsible for what happened but am responsible for how I react
to what happened.

_____ I am now ready to admit that the way I am feeling is a
natural response to what has happened.

_____ I understand that beating up on myself helps no one and
contributes nothing positive.

_____ I am ready to begin having more positive thoughts about
my family's future.

_____ I am ready to find new ways to meet my needs and
nurture myself.

Anger's Dangers

One of my first terrible rushes of rage came without warning, and it was so strong that I can still feel it today. It was frightening to feel it growing inside my chest, constricting my breathing, sending blood rushing to my face. A therapist had scolded me for being too unrealistic about my expectations for Dale's recovery and for encouraging him to set a goal of returning to work as an engineer.

"He has to accept his disability," she said. "He can't go on expecting to go back to engineering."

My response, unlike the meek agreement I had offered up in the past, was immediate and sharp. She was saying that we had to give up, a response so alien to my philosophy of life that I could not—would not—accept it. She was supposed to be helping him, not telling him to give up. I struggled for control as I told her that I would not give up and I would not tell Dale to. And as I talked, the other therapists in the room looked at each other and smiled. They had just classified me as denying. To them, I was being unreasonable. Perhaps I was, but the anger was satisfying. Who said these people were always right?

Anger is a powerful motivator if it can be focused and controlled. Like any other emotion that families of brain injury go through, it needs to be guided and understood.

My focus for anger was, initially, on my own life, which seemed hopelessly confused and out of control. I felt betrayed, and I wanted some revenge. Much as prisoners of war maintain their sanity and sense of self-worth by performing small acts of rebellion that may go unnoticed by their keepers, I was determined to regain some control.

I was tired of being a victim. The anger gave me enough energy to retake control of my life. It enabled me to redirect the energy I'd been using up with guilt and to detach myself from other people's judgments. It enabled me to hang a garage door and to stop punishing myself for my inability to motivate Dale. It enabled me to threaten him with arrest if he hurt me anymore.

Within the grief process, anger can be a truly healing process. Anger allows you to turn all the emotion outward, so that the damage accrues elsewhere. It doesn't take away all the guilt or denial, but it certainly frees you.

Many people dredge up their anger from the very bottom of their souls and spew it outward on everyone. I was very resentful of other families who were living a normal life. I thought it was awful that they could go on as if nothing had happened when my family's survival was threatened on every side. It wasn't fair.

And I was very resentful of those friends who disappeared. They had abandoned us. They didn't call. They didn't stop by. They didn't send cards. I was resentful toward family members who, after the first month or so, wrote us out of their lives. And I was angry with those who always had ideas about how I could do a better job of something or other.

I was, of course, angry with the medical profession. I was angry that they could presume to decide between life and death when they didn't know what the life would be like. I was angry that they presumed to tell me how I should feel and what I should accept.

I was angry with Dale for everything.

I was even angry with my kids (12 and 14 years old) for not being more understanding and trying harder to help.

You may be one of the people who will be upset with the idea that I could be angry with Dale, a victim who could not help what happened to him. Some will be offended that I was angry with my children. But I was. It seems cruel to say so now. But it seems even more cruel and unreasonable to actually feel that way.

But who said I had to be reasonable? My life was in disarray. I was down and out. I was grieving not only for Dale's lost health and dreams, but for my own and my children's lost dreams. I deserved better. We all deserved better. We've been cheated out of something that everyone around us seemed to have.

Anger is mobilizing. It allows you to protest. To rebel against what's unfair, you have to be angry. Righteous anger gives you a certain dignity. Remember the old saying, "I won't take that lying down?" Anger pulls you to your feet. Anger gives you the strength to stand up and fight back.

Focusing your anger is the challenge before you. Take a piece of paper out and write down all your resentments. This simple exercise may help you understand where your anger truly lies. I would guess that all the pages of anger could be summer up fairly simply.

"Things are not the way they are supposed to be."

"What's happened isn't fair."

Once you can focus your anger on these fairly simple ideas, you can use the energy to build a new life despite the tragedy that has battered you down.

My willingness to be assertive and to be decisive came out of anger. I was angry enough to demand change, something I'd rarely done for myself before. And out of that came a certain understanding of my own strength. I grew in my anger. I developed empathy for other angry people and I could accept rather than reject their anger. I learned to look past their hostility until I could see their pain. I began to rebuild.

This book came out of anger. I wanted information about the struggle of families of brain injured people to be available. I knew that most of us were not willing or not able to ask for help in our struggle. Books are private and less expensive than therapy. And they are less threatening. I can read about anger and be more comfortable than I would be if I was sitting in the same room with a therapist and baring my soul. I wanted other people to have a book to read to help them understand what was happening to them.

EXERCISE

Anger is a powerful motivator. It can be used to hurt yourself or others, or it can be used as a tool for positive change. To better understand and guide your anger, list in your notebook, the person, events and circumstances about who or which you are very angry, and then in the note what they did to make you angry. (Example: My doctor. He doesn't call me back as quickly as he should when I have important questions.) If you don't have enough room to list everything, use a separate piece of paper.

EXERCISE

In your notebook, list one or more things that you would like to do to express your anger. (Example: Tell my doctor what a jerk he is and that I'm not going to pay him.) Write as much as you'd like and, if necessary, use another piece of paper.

EXERCISE

As one who has intimate knowledge of what coping with a brain-injured family member is all about, I can sympathize strongly with almost any action you may have listed. However, very often our initial desires in response to anger aren't appropriate actions to actually take. It would be a good idea to list in your notebook some of the likely consequences to you and your family if you were to carry out any of the actions you wrote down.

EXERCISE

Okay, now let's talk about what you can do that WILL help solve some problems. Use a page or two in your notebook to begin making a concrete plan to get control of those things that are out of control now. Be modest in the beginning. You have lots on your plate and may only be able to address one or two of these issues.

Depression

Sometimes I begin to weep at the silliest things. Sad movies are certain faucet openers. So are some happy movies. The sight of a child being loudly reprimanded in the grocery store can make me teary. The lonely isolation of some teenagers makes me cry. The wary look on the face of an alcoholic's wife brings tears to my eyes.

One night when I had to work late and arrived home long after everyone had gone to bed, I found a note on the garage door from my son.

"I love you, Mom," it said.

I took it off the door, held it tightly against my chest and sobbed.

I have to be careful that I don't laugh too hard because such a release of emotion can mean a spilling of tears and strange looks from people who wonder about my sanity.

But I'm happy that I can finally shed tears because for a very long time I could not. I felt like an empty shell. My sadness was so deep that I couldn't bring anything up to the surface. The pain had beaten me. The only thing could find inside was an occasional flash of anger.

This was not what I expected grief to feel like. Somehow I thought there would be more crying—mourning. But there was nothing inside me. Only the great, overwhelming emptiness. I couldn't see the tunnel, let alone the light at the end.

When you live with brain injury, depression comes and goes. Every time you see a little progress in your brain injured family member, the depression lifts a little. But as soon as a plateau hits, you plunge back into the depths. Every financial setback and every new challenge drags you back down.

That's why depression in your family can be a serious challenge. Fighting it off takes supernatural energy. When someone is seriously depressed, it is easy for that person to lose sight of a goal. It's difficult to see a bright future. It's easier to look for relief in drugs and alcohol.

And it isn't always easy to spot depression. Convinced that my son was experiencing very serious depression and aware that he was being seduced by drugs and alcohol, I took him to see our family doctor, a man well-schooled in the problems of teenagers. The problem with Mike, however, wasn't normal. The doctor has a very nice questionnaire for his teenage patients that helps him pinpoint what's bothering the kids. But Mike knew all the answers. Like most of us who are dealing with the tragedy of brain injury, he could fool the family doctor. "It's not me. I'm worried about my dad." That's the correct response. It immediately takes the problem off our own shoulders and puts it somewhere else.

"I'm fine," we argue. "I don't have a problem. I'm just a little tired." We know that people will readily understand *that*.

But we are the problem. We're dealing with more than any normal person should have to. That's very depressing. We need to admit that we are depressed before we can find ways to get out of the muck.

Going about the daily routine is an important step. If we let things go, we just get more depressed. Two days' dishes sitting in the sink are more depressing than one day's. Taking a shower and combing our hair will make us feel more human and more capable even if we don't *feel* strong enough to lift a comb.

Work was a salvation for me when I was caught in the deepest depths of depression. I had to get dressed and go to work. I had to talk to people, write stories and make plans. And while I was doing that, I couldn't think about what was wrong with my life.

My children also gave me strength. I had to make dinner for them. I had to go to concerts, talk to their friends and help with their homework.

You can hold depression at bay for a while with the things you have to do, but sooner or later you will have to reorganize your life so that you are replacing some of the tasks you have to do with things you want to do.

Everyone needs to have an escape from the drudgery of brain injury. Everyone needs a little pleasure. Even though you are financially strapped, you must find ways to give yourself a lift. A few moments of conversation with an understanding friend will help you stay afloat for days or even weeks. A cup of hot chocolate fixed just the way you like it in a nice china cup may relax you just enough that you can cope for another day. A 15-minute walk alone or a few minutes in your garden may drive away the blues.

All of these small devices will gradually help to get rid of the overwhelming depression that can envelop your family. Take pleasures where you find them. You deserve them. What you are feeling is very normal. We all get discouraged and depressed when we are dealing with head injury. What's most important is not to become so overwhelmed that we can't cope. Let the anger work against depression. Kick it in the knee and punch it in the nose. Like everything else in brain injury, it's a struggle.

EXERCISE

Depression can sneak up on you. You may not realize that you are seriously depressed until you find yourself at the bottom of a very deep emotional pit. Here are some the more common clues to depression. How many of the feelings listed below apply to you?

_____ I have trouble sleeping.

_____ I find myself wanting to sleep all the time.

_____ My sense of humor is gone.

_____ I don't seem to have much purpose in life anymore.

_____ I am easily irritated by things that didn't bother me before.

_____ I find myself withdrawing from people I used to enjoy.

_____ I have trouble thinking about the future.

_____ There are times I think it would be easier if I just died.

_____ I am so drained of energy I can hardly force myself out of bed in the morning.

_____ Nothing I do seems to make a difference or matter to anyone.

_____ I just don't feel good physically anymore.

_____ I'm drinking too much or using too many pills.

_____ I think the most horrible things.

EXERCISE

Don't be surprised if you recognized most, if not all, of the possibilities listed above. Dealing with the consequences of a severe head injury to a member of your family is one of the most difficult challenges you may ever have to face. If you are just beginning to face the reality of your situation, frankly, you would be less than normal if you were not expressing the kinds of symptoms and feelings described on the previous page. There are many ways to cope and what worked for me may not work for you. If you find yourself unable to pull yourself out of the pit of depression, remember that there are many ways to treat and overcome depression. You can't always do it alone, but there are many people to help you. Counselors and physicians can be invaluable.

Please let me reassure you that:

1. Most people experience these kinds of feelings when confronted with this kind of severe loss.

2. When you are feeling severe depression, it is a good time to seek professional assistance from a trained counselor, clergyperson or physician. Depression is the result of a chemical imbalance in the brain. Not everyone needs medication for this problem, but it can be an effective treatment in many cases.

3. Scientists believe that acute depression is an indication that the brain is changing itself in order to cope with new circumstances. Because this is true, it important to realize that depression may not be alleviated by the power of positive thinking. Counseling and/or medication may be necessary. See your doctor or counselor.

4. It is very important that you find some time, even if only a few moments each day, to take yourself out of the environment in which you are coping with your family's immediate needs. Please make a few moments to engage in some activity that will serve as a reminder that the world is a larger place than merely a bedroom or home dominated by the needs of a particular individual.

5. As soon as possible, expand the time you are claiming for yourself by making new friends; finding new activities; going to new and different places; networking with people in similar straits; learning all you can about how others have coped with head injury; seeking information to help you define your future; and thinking about how your new circumstance relate to your own purpose in life.

Acceptance

I don't know exactly when or how my acceptance began to take form. I believe it probably started about the time I began to take more control over my life. It began when I could say, "Well, I can't stand this for another year, but I can probably get through this week." And with that assurance, I could pull my nose away from my grindstone long enough to see that there were others who had much more difficult problems to solve. When I could see that I wasn't the only person in the world with problems, I began to feel less that our family had been singled out—to feel less alone. Piece by piece I began to put my life in order.

With that control, my self-esteem began to grow stronger again. I felt brave enough to meet the challenges. I felt sorry, in a way, for people who'd never had major problems because they didn't understand how lucky they were.

It took years for that to evolve into my belief that happiness is an attitude—not having all your dreams fulfilled. Meeting challenges is rewarding in itself. Life is not "living happily ever after." Life is simply living—whatever that may bring.

It's pretty hard to deny that something terrible has happened to your family. Yet accepting the enormity of the tragedy is harder than most people think. Because you may grieve about this head injury for a long time, you can only accept where you are at any particular time. You have to take a little snapshot of your life and ask if you are accepting what's real— what's in the snapshot right now.

What acceptance really means is taking your life off hold and getting on with it. If your house burns down you will probably grieve for its loss, but when you have settled into a new house and learned your new address by memory, you will have probably accepted what's happened.

Families of brain injury victims have to rebuild more than a house. They have to rebuild their lives and their family relationships. Since that is a constantly changing process, acceptance of brain injury takes a long time. But one morning you may wake up feeling like your life is peaceful again. You may have set up a new set of goals and are working to achieve them. You no longer think of yourself as a family devastated by tragedy. You've accepted. You still have pain, guilt, depression and anger, but they are coincidental to your life, not the very center of it. When that happens I hope you can offer a helping hand to others who are struggling to achieve acceptance.

Not long ago a friend called and began to cry as she told me that her father, who had been ill for a very long time, would probably not live through the week. As we talked, she poured out her grief, and we talked about how difficult it was to face up to such loss. Before she hung up, she said, "Oh, Marilyn, you're so wise. You always know what to say to help me get through the pain."

Her assessment made me a little uncomfortable. I don't feel very wise. I'm still learning to deal with my own pain, but I know what she's feeling and I can certainly empathize with her. If wisdom comes from experience, then perhaps I will, someday, grow wise. That's something to look forward to. But for the time being, I'm happy that my experience and my acceptance of loss can help her deal with hers.

Self Care

It was about 9:30 on a weeknight when the man knocked on the door. My friend Marty and I were working on a project in my office. It had already been a stressful week with three freelance assignments due and a newsletter project at work falling behind deadline. We were short of money, and Mike's first installment on his college tuition was due. Dale had recently fallen off his bike, breaking his wrist and hitting his head on the pavement, destroying nearly a year's progress in his speech despite the protection his helmet gave him.

When I answered the door, the man handed me a summons. Surprise, we were being sued over a traffic accident in which Dale was involved two years earlier. The insurance company hadn't told us there was any dispute at all.

I panicked. If my friend hadn't been there to carefully read the summons and help me understand what it was about, I'm not sure what I would have done. I didn't sleep for days. My blood pressure stayed too high and I was stressed out.

I've read a lot about stress management in my search for ways to relieve the stress of that kind of day and the enormous task of caring for my head injured husband. Every book I've read has a suggestion that goes something like this: Imagine that you had nothing to do for a whole day and you could fill that day with anything you wanted to do. Think of what you could do for yourself and act on it.

When you live with head injury you may not be able to imagine what a day all to yourself would be like. I've tried it. This is what happens to me:

Oh wow! A day for myself.
I could balance the checkbook and
fold the clothes that have been
lying in the laundry basket for a
week (okay, two weeks). Then I'd
probably have time to straighten
up the basement or clean some
cupboards or file some of those
documents for the disability
commission or get the cans to the
recycle center, or get the kids some
new jeans or...

It makes me too tired to think about it. I'm sure you know what I'm talking about. I simply can't imagine so much time being wasted on me. When there are so many demands, there just doesn't seem to be any way for everyone to have time for themselves. But if we don't take care of ourselves, our family relationships will suffer and the stress will only increase. This can lead to a family breakup—something we're trying to avoid.

Finding relief for stress when you're dealing with brain injury is difficult. Every family undergoes significant stress. It's a fact of life. But most stress management systems are geared to normal stress loads. They take into account higher than normal periods of stress but not the continual bombardment of highly stressful conditions that accompany brain injury.

When someone in a family is brain injured, stress grows exponentially. You don't even have your normal stress patterns to lean on because radical changes take place in the household.

There are fairly common signs that signal a stress overload. Although some of the signs may occur naturally in anyone's lifetime, when they occur in progression, or all together, they may be a distress signal from your soul. This is caregiver burnout and it's serious.

To others you may appear compulsive and a little bit crazy, but it's very common for a caregiver to believe that she or he is the only one who can do anything right for the brain-injured family member. After all, that person asks for you, depends on you, and expects you to be there. But it's true that we can carry it too far. When we are heading for burnout, we may begin to demand too much of ourselves. Dinner must be fixed just so. The sheets must be changed every Monday no matter what else needs to be done.

Because we can feel the inner weakness, we redouble our efforts to be responsible because we're afraid we might forget something important. We become so intent on getting everything done, and done perfectly, that we lose track of whether it really needs to be done at all.

This is a hard symptom to catch, and often we are pretty far into the burnout cycle before we realize we're in trouble. The reasons are simple. Our brain-injured family member requires a great deal of care and supervision. It's rare that the primary caregiver isn't overtaxed. Even if we have help from other family members, it's difficult to recognize when we step over the line from occasionally demanding too much of ourselves because it's absolutely necessary, to the point where we continually demand too much.

Most of us pass into this part of the burnout cycle without realizing it. The demands are so great that we almost have to be compulsive about getting tasks done in order to keep our lives rolling.

So how in the world will we find time for ourselves? In a family dealing with head injury, everyone needs so much care that the primary caregiver (and there is usually only one) puts herself or himself on the bottom of the list of priorities.

There is so much to do for everyone. We kicked ourselves into emotional and physical overdrive when our family member first became injured and that worked pretty well. The problem is that since head injury is such a long-term problem, we keep ourselves at double time, sometimes for years.

In the first five years after Dale's surgery, we went through an amazing number of changes in our lives. My children moved from elementary and middle school to high school and college. We drastically altered our lifestyle to match our reduced income. We experienced complete role changes within the family and totally changed relationships between family members. We changed an entire set of relationships with people outside the family. I went through several career moves and I shifted my priorities from being a stay-at-home mom with a part-time career to supporting the family and providing a college education for the children.

All these changes were piled on top of the emotional struggle with grief, anger and depression. It didn't leave me much time for relaxation or pleasure.

I think some of my compromises have been foolish, now that I can look back with a little detachment. A year or so after Dale's injury, I went to a professional conference at a nearby ski resort. I really looked forward to getting away from the hectic office, hearing new ideas and comparing notes with others in my field. But what would I do with Dale while I was gone? The kids were able to stay with friends, but Dale refused to stay with anyone else, and I couldn't leave him at home alone or with the children because of his unpredictability, clumsiness and intellectual confusion. While my company was paying for my conference expenses, they wouldn't cover paying someone to come and stay in the house for three days.

My solution was to take him with me. Since he spent most of his time watching television, I was sure he would be content. There was a swimming pool, hot tub, and the television in our room, and he could attend the conference lunches and dinners with me. It seemed like a decent compromise.

But there was no way for me to relax there. At the end of our meetings, I found Dale waiting for me outside the conference room. He wanted to go somewhere or he needed something, so instead of taking a break between sessions, I took care of him. He tired easily and wanted to go back to the room immediately after dinner. But he wanted me to go with him and if I wouldn't, he stayed, and I would feel uncomfortable as he weaved in his chair and became less and less coherent. I had very little time to participate in discussions or soak up new ideas. I ended up coming home more tired than when I'd left, and feeling very resentful. When someone would comment on how nice it was that I'd been able to get away, I wanted to cry. Still, I felt like I'd done things the way they should be done. Dale came first. My needs were secondary.

Most of us don't give our own needs much credence or weight. I had a very real need to get away from the constant demands of work and caring for my family, but I couldn't see my own need was just as important as Dale's need to be included. I believe I might have been able to find an alternative solution, if I had given my needs any importance. As it was, I continued to deplete my reserves. To do something just for myself seemed too selfish.

The very real demands of caring for a brain-injured person are enormous. That's why it is so difficult to moderate stress within the family. What we have to remember is that stress is a killer. Research shows very direct links between stress and heart attack, stress and cancer, stress and stroke, stress and suicide, stress and substance abuse. Stress also breaks up families. It can cause an emotional depression that is contagious within the family and fatal to our ability to cope with problems. We become indecisive, irritable and unable to judge our priorities in a logical manner. We might be able to recognize approaching burnout at this point, but we're likely to dismiss it as exhaustion, something we'll take care of just as soon as the pressure lets up and we have a little time.

But it doesn't happen that way.

When we are overstressed and still have much to do, the easiest thing to do is deny the little voice in the back of your head that's telling you you're in trouble. If we pretend we don't feel the pain or the exhaustion, it doesn't exist for us. As caregivers we fall into this very easily because we know certain tasks have to be done even if we don't feel like doing them or if we're too tired to attempt them.

I can remember coming home from work one evening, a distance of about 20 miles, and teaching myself to deny my own physical exhaustion. Before I left the office I was having trouble keeping my eyes open. I had to read the papers in front of me several times before they made sense. Once on the freeway, the gentle hum of the tires and the open road made it easy for my eyes to slip closed. Twice I stopped the car, got out and walked around the car a few times, and took some deep breaths. I climbed back in and, in a few minutes, my eyes would slip closed again. I couldn't imagine how I was going to get home this way. I knew I had to fix dinner and then attend a meeting at the school. In desperation and with the air conditioner cranked up to its highest speed, I tried some visualization. I imagined myself in an icy lake, swimming to the raft just beyond my reach. Amazingly, instead of ending up in a car accident, it worked! I got home and fixed dinner, chatted with the kids about their homework and went to the meeting. I even sat through it without falling asleep and got home again. I'd found my own kind of hallucinogen—cheap and legal, but perhaps nearly as dangerous. All I had to do was ignore what my body was telling me and override my logical mind with a false image. I'd disengaged from reality.

While we all ignore our tired feelings occasionally, as a caregiver it's very easy to step over the edge and ignore everything we feel. During an interview with the mother of a two-year-old sexual assault victim, I suddenly felt as though I was looking in through a window. I am usually very empathetic, and this kind of interview should have evoked a deep emotional reaction in me. But that day I could feel absolutely nothing. It seemed so strange that I wondered if I was dreaming. After the interview, I blamed my inability to empathize on the mother who had trusted her child to a near stranger. It wasn't me that was having a problem, it was that careless mother who had trusted her child with a near-stranger.

Back in the office, that rationalization frightened me enough that I had to look at what was happening to my emotions. But like many other caregivers, even though I knew something was wrong, I didn't associate it with my own inability to cope.

I found myself putting on a false face every morning and forcing myself to act clever and cheerful even though I felt miserable. I relied more and more on other people's research in my stories because I was too tired and withdrawn to make the effort to research the stories myself. I didn't want to answer the phone. I began to doubt my abilities and to fear being found out.

One friend, who was going through a similar stage of burnout because of alcoholism and family problems, told me about waiting for the "fraud wagon" to arrive and carry him away. He expected that any moment someone would come bursting through his office door, point at him and scream "FRAUD!" as everyone turned to stare and nod. Sometimes I wished that fraud wagon would hurry to my office because if I was discovered, someone else would have to take over all my problems.

But it wasn't just at work that I shut down my emotions. I shut them down everywhere. I stopped hearing what the kids were telling me although I appeared to be listening. I stopped caring if Dale did his therapy, although I asked about it and reminded him to do it. I lay on the couch after everyone else had gone to bed and stared at the television without seeing or hearing.

Too many of us who are dealing with brain injury don't allow ourselves to see that we are burning out. We know we are tired, but we can't see any way out. We develop a state of emotion where all we can say is, "I can't—but I must." Nothing becomes as important as the task of caring for our brain-injured family member and our family, of getting to work, of doing what must be done.

If we are dealing at the same time with the guilt and anger of the grief process, we may lose our sense of priorities. How can we not lose our way in such a circumstance? So we stop talking to others because they always have advice to give—can't they see you have no choices anymore? We find fault and blame for the smallest irritation. We snap at salesclerks. We have attitude adjustment sessions at the nearest bar. I began keeping candy bars in my desk drawer and after every stressful phone call or interview, or when deadline pressures grew, I would stuff myself with chocolate. At home I watched television and ignored what needed to be done around the house. I just wanted someone to take over for me because I couldn't do it anymore!

Of course, none of the destructive cures helped. They only made things worse. I drank too much, put on 30 pounds, and I grew alienated from the people and things I loved the most. I was burned out. As a matter of fact, I'm sure my very soul was scorched around the edges.

The Three P's to Stress Reduction

Perspective

The thing that bothered me most about my family's life was the chaos we seemed to be involved in. I couldn't keep it together no matter how much I tried. I wrote list after list of reminders and then, pressed for time, I forgot to look at the lists. I forgot appointments. I arrived either early or late for meetings. I forgot the names of my very best friends when trying to introduce them. The laundry went undone. The dishes piled up in the sink. The car's oil wasn't changed. I ignored the bills.

And yet, when we visited friends who had hectic schedules, they seemed to be in control and their lives seemed to be running quite smoothly. What was I doing wrong? Was I just too unorganized and incompetent to get my act together?

No. I was just trying to live with brain injury in the family.

A pickup truck bouncing along a rugged mountain trail doesn't ride nearly as quietly as the same truck zipping along a newly paved road. A jigsaw puzzle with a thousand pieces is not as easy to put together as a jigsaw puzzle with only 10 pieces.

Why do we feel that our lives, which have become much more complicated and difficult than "normal" lives, should operate with the same kind of organization? It's just not possible. Since so many new stressful things have been dumped on us, we have to get rid of those inner stresses that we've always been able to ignore before.

How? By simplifying.

A lot of the stress that we feel in life comes from little inner voices nagging at us. There are those "shoulds" that your mother instilled in you, the "musts" that you learned from your father and quite a few "don'ts" that you got from everyone else. Until we gain a little perspective, all those voices inside sound like laws when, in fact, many have no practical value in our lives.

Thank goodness you can learn to sort out the voices and silence those that don't belong.

First, make a list of all the "shoulds" on your list. Then take a step back and try to evaluate whose "shoulds" they are. Who are you trying to please? Are you staying up until midnight to make sure the house is spotless and floors waxed because your Aunt Florence always said a messy house was the mark of a slothful person? Are you working two jobs because your father said a man who couldn't provide luxuries for his family wasn't a successful man? Why are you involved in that bridge club? Why do you insist on fixing fancy meals? Why must the grass be greener than anyone else's?

Because your life is so much more complex now, you must decide which of the "shoulds" and "musts" in your life are important. If you are doing something that is difficult to work into your schedule and that makes you resentful and angry, decide whether it's really important in your life right now. If it's not, cross if off the list. If you are hearing someone else's voice telling you what to do, turn down the volume and listen to your heart and mind.

When you have been able to eliminate all but the most essential responsibilities, think about what it is that you've been foregoing in order to accomplish those things that you've just crossed off your list. Have you denied yourself time with your family? A chance to talk about your problems with someone who can help? What can you substitute in your life that you truly need? And yes, what would you do if you had a day to yourself? Would it be healing to explore that idea?

Before brain injury came into our lives, we made it a point to eat our evening meal at the dinner table together. So when Dale began cooking, he expected everyone to sit down together when he had dinner ready. There were two problems with that. The first problem was that he wasn't able to predict when he could have dinner ready because he was still struggling with the organizational task of preparing food. The second problem was that as our children grew older and became active in outside activities, they seemed to have conflicting schedules. While this is a problem for most families of teenagers, it was more difficult for us because of Dale's rigid expectations.

At first I tried to require everyone to be home and ready for dinner at 6:30 and to stay there until we'd eaten. That created a lot of turmoil and resentment because if Dale wasn't able to get dinner ready by then, the kids might be late to whatever activity they were participating in. If I excused them or fixed a sandwich for them and sent them off, Dale would be furious because he felt he was wasting his time and effort cooking for only part of the family.

So, tired of the conflict, I tried to explain to Dale that it was in the family's interest for him to be more flexible, and I held fast to that analysis despite his angry tantrums. Enforcing that old tradition was only creating more stress for everyone for no practical reason. The family's true need was to spend some time talking and sharing the day's happenings. There were other times for that. So Dale fixed dinner with an eye to getting it on the table at a specific time and the kids tried to make it. If they didn't, everyone knew their dinner would be in the refrigerator ready to heat up when they got home.

What a relief! The yelling and resentment was reduced exponentially. No one left the table with his or her dinner sitting like a rock at stomach's bottom because there had been a fight at the dinner table. If everyone made it to dinner, the conversation was pleasant. And with a lessening of tension, everyone talked more easily at other times too.

It seemed so simple once I let go of the "should" of our old life habits.

In the same way, I used to be embarrassed if one of our friends arrived and the house was a mess. I knew my children must be ashamed when their friends came into such a messy place. I thought I must look like a terrible mother to them, but try as I might, I simply couldn't get it all done. Housecleaning wasn't the first, or even thirtieth, priority of my day, but the guilt was killing me just the same. What would everyone else say about us?

It finally occurred to me that if the kids did care (and they didn't seem to) they could help clean up before their friends came. They were okay with that, it turned out, believe it or not. And the guilt went away, leaving me with more time to think about positive changes I could make.

These are stresses I should have dealt with a long time before. But just realizing that they were unnecessary gave me simple remedies to the incredible stress I was feeling with all the extra responsibilities of head injury. I suppose I had been operating on automatic. I had been listing to those voices inside for so long, I didn't recognize my own voice crying out for something different.

Please, reclaim your own emotions. Listen closely for your own voice in the pulpit and do only what that personal voice says is necessary or authentically pleasing to you. Dump the excess baggage you've been carrying around and begin to travel light. Allow yourself a little perspective on your situation. Your life is different now than it was before. Reevaluate your priorities in relationship to those changes, and modify your expectations accordingly.

People

I don't think my family would have survived the stress we've experience without the people who have been here to support us. Those people include family, friends, therapists, doctors, and other families of head injured people. Yes, many people let us down. But some special ones didn't. They are the ones who have helped us learn to cope.

Let me tell you about "the breakfast club." Before he was injured, Dale and several other engineers got up early every Friday morning and met for breakfast before going to work. Although they were friends and colleagues, Dale would not have considered them his closest friends. But more than five years later, those same men were picking him up for breakfast every Friday morning and continued until he asked them to stop. They were a lifeline for him, a link which made him feel more accepted. Most of the people he would earlier have considered to be closer friends have disappeared.

I have been similarly blessed with friends and family who accept what happened to our family, who were there when we desperately needed support and who didn't make judgements about the way we conducted our very different life.

Those people who understand are emotional lifelines. They helped us keep our perspective. Without them, it would have been simple to withdraw into our shell and become reclusive, angry and bitter.

One family I talked with has done just that, and I'm not sure if they will come out again. They are extremely angry at the response they've gotten from health professions, family and friends. They expected a great deal of support and found that others just couldn't bear the strain of seeing their child so gravely injured and a family coming apart at the seams. As a result, this family has become very insular. They only rely on immediate family members or paid professional of whom they are very critical. They don't socialize because they don't want to have their son stared at or misunderstood. They are very bitter about what has happened to them, and everyone in the house is tense and critical. It they are not already burned out and heading for a family breakup, they are well on their way. I understand how they got to this point, but I hope they can find their way out again.

I'm not sure how many families survive their incredible string of crises. But here's one clue. Every one of the families who seem to be coping well appears to have a strong spiritual life. Some belong to organized churches while others have their own private spiritual strengths to carry them through each crisis. But it is easy to see that we need somebody or something to lean on when we're dealing with brain injury. It's just too difficult to do it alone—and we don't have to. There are all kinds of resources for us if we can look past our own fears and reach out to someone for help.

Don't isolate yourself. Don't try to keep all your pain inside or try to cope all by yourself. There are people who understand

and who are very willing to help. It may be easiest to find that help in your local support group because the people there have been through the same experiences. They can give you both emotional support and practical suggestions. Most of us who are dealing with a brain injured family member occasionally become overwhelmed with our problems, no matter how long we've been dealing with it.

One of our support group members came to a meeting a few years ago on a night when we had a guest speaker in to talk about stress management.

"What do you do when your family member acts inappropriately and you're not sure he can resolve it himself or you need to step in?" one member asked the speaker. Stress had become especially heavy the weekend before when the family had been shopping and the brain-injured family member had gotten into a dispute with a store owner. "You want him to learn the consequences of his actions, but you also don't want him to hurt anyone," the questioner continued. "I never know if I'm doing the right thing."

The expert stumbled around with possible solutions, and I watched our member's face fall as he slowly realized that the speaker had no help to offer. But after the program, another group member put his arm around the man and they discussed the problem for a few moments. I could almost see the man's shoulders straighten as the other group member shared his experience. There is no substitute for true understanding and insight.

I admit I fought going to the support group at first because I thought it was silly to waste my time when Dale would be totally recovered in a few months. Most of us feel that way at first, when we're denying the worst and hoping for the best. I went at first because Dale wanted to go. We then began to participate more frequently because I needed the understanding and support I found there.

There are other kinds of support that you may need and should ask for. Sometimes our emotional struggle grows to overwhelming proportions, and we need to seek professional counseling. This is no time to be stoic. Go to your minister or a professional counselor and ask for help. Don't isolate yourself from this kind of support because of your pride or because of a feeling that only weak or crazy people have to see a counselor. If you were struggling with an overwhelming accounting problem, wouldn't you seek out an accountant? If you were faced with a legal problem, wouldn't you talk to a lawyer? Professional counseling is no different. It serves a need.

Many times your hospital social worker or rehabilitation department staffer can offer other resources, other forms of support ranging from medical to financial. These people all want to help. But we have to ask for their help before they can give it. There is no weakness in leaning on other people when you are in distress.

Pleasure

All work and no play makes Jack a dull boy. It also may drive Jack to a nervous breakdown.

All work and no play makes Jill a pretty boring girl too. She may also become an alcoholic or develop an eating disorder.

We all need to have a little fun—a little pleasure to balance the pain we've been through since our family member was brain-injured. The problem is finding time or resources for our pleasure.

Perspective has a place here. When we think of pleasure many of us think of a week's vacation in the mountains, or going out dancing, or visiting Disneyland. That may be a little too grand for our stressed-out pocketbooks, and it might also be impossible for us to get away from our responsibilities for any length of time. But that doesn't mean we can't find little pleasures to keep us going.

One very active mother of a brain-injured person finds pleasure in a way that would never work for me. Because she works with people all day long at her job and is surrounded by family at home, her special treat is to be all alone.

That doesn't mean she sits in a corner somewhere and thinks about her problems, however. She renovates houses in her spare time (what there is of it). The hammering and sawing and the stripping of paint are her own form of therapy. First she tears away the old shabby parts and then rebuilds with something clean and renewed. Whether or not she sees the renovation as symbolic of her family's struggle to be whole again is not important. She is alone with her work. She may return to her family physically exhausted, but her spirit is renewed and she will have new strength with which to cope.

Much of my work life is solitary. I sit at my computer and type, or I read or research. At home I'm a sponge. I absorb myself in everyone else's life, hearing about school or making dental appointments or discussing whatever problems have come up. My pleasure comes from talking with people outside the family. A quick lunch with friends from a local newspaper revives me. An hour's conversation with one or two women who have similar career goals is exhilarating. Time with a close friend is nurturing. The laughter and tears that we share provide patching material for my tattered soul.

One man finds pleasure in rebuilding old cars. Others play basketball or go fishing. One farm wife leaves the house and stands in the middle of the fields just enjoying the sights, smells and sounds of the land.

Pleasure doesn't have to be grandiose. I have two strawberry patches in my garden. One is large and produces strawberries for freezing or for desserts. The other patch is small and doesn't produce a great number of strawberries. However, the strawberries it does produce are exquisitely sweet, particularly when warmed by the sun and washed off by a garden hose. This is MY strawberry patch. The rest of the family doesn't care much for "plain old strawberries," so I save the berries from this small patch just for me. It feels incredibly luxurious to pop those delicacies into my mouth on a hot summer day when I'm overwhelmed with responsibilities. I don't know why that makes me feel better, but it does. Perhaps just doing something special for myself makes me feel a bit more special.

We all need to feel important. When a member of our family is brain-injured, and all the family's attention is focused on him or her, everyone else may feel put upon or neglected.

In a study a few years ago, babies in orphanages who were fed in their cribs with bottle propped on pillows were significantly less healthy than babies who were picked up, rocked and cuddled while they were fed by an adult. So it is with our families. We all need pleasure and stimulation to keep us healthy. We think better, we respond better to other people, and we are more cooperative if we can find a little pleasure in our lives.

At first, after our family member is brain-injured, finding any time for pleasure seems nearly impossible. This is when it's so necessary to find the small pleasures of life. Working in the

92

garden, a bouquet of flowers for the table, a marvelous brew of freshly ground coffee—any of these little pleasures might revive your flagging spirits and energy. Allowing yourself $10 worth of long distance phone calls during a month to a supportive friend could be worth a fortune to you and may help you avoid severe burnout. Everyone finds pleasure in different ways. I found the little extra time I needed by taking time I felt was wasted watching television. Another person might want to mop the kitchen floor every other week instead of every week so that she can watch something special on television that she is really interested in. If you just place yourself a little higher on your list of priorities, you'll find that you can make time to do something nice for yourself.

It may be hard to do at first. You may feel guilty for spending time and money to do something just for your own pleasure. You wouldn't have felt guilty if you were doing it for your head-injured family member, but somehow it doesn't seem right that you're doing it for yourself. This is a major stumbling block that will take concentrated effort and self-talk to get through. Head injury is a family problem. Every member of the family needs special care because everyone has been injured.

I can almost see a primary caregiver in this situation beginning to panic at the thought of all those people needing extra care. That's the problem with us as caregivers. We're always trying to make everyone else happy at our own expense. That's nice, but eventually our own resources are going to dry up. We'll be empty and angry because we haven't given ourselves any nourishing pleasure to keep our life worth living.

If you can't see your way clear to allow yourself some pleasure just for your own good, do it for the rest of the family.

A caregiver who's given away everything can't provide much care for the rest of the family.

One family learned the value of pleasure this way. They had been having a very difficult month both financially and emotionally. Their brain-injured family member wasn't making much progress as far as anyone could tell, and everyone was tired and resentful of all the demands that had been dropped into their laps. As they stood in the kitchen after work discussing their problems, the mother announced that they had only $20 left in the checking account. The next few days, dinners would be peanut butter sandwiches or soup, she told them, because she wasn't going to the grocery store until payday. Tears glittered in her eyes as she turned away.

For a moment her husband sat pensively looking from one member of the quiet, depressed family to the other. Suddenly, he stood up, put on his hat and left. He returned after a half hour with a bag of groceries. In the bag was $20 worth of steaks. He seated his wife at the table and proceeded to produce a steak dinner with baked potatoes, and tossed salad from the last of the refrigerated lettuce, slightly brown around the edges. His family grumbled about the extravagance, but he ignored them and sang a silly song as he grilled the steak. By the time dinner was over, they were laughing at a round of knock-knock jokes and hugging each other.

This family remembers that steak dinner as a special event that brought the family closer together and nourished their souls as well as their bodies. It was the best use of those last few dollars that they could possibly have found.

While I'm not advocating that anyone throw financial caution to the wind, it's still good to remember that whether it's a special dinner or a walk around the block, pleasure can serve as a bridge over the worst of times. We must place pleasure high on our list of priorities if we expect our families to remain healthy.

When Families Falter

I often think back to a conversation I had with an associate when Dale was still in the hospital. She stopped beside my desk and inquired how he was doing and when I expected him home. I was fairly honest when I told her he was better but could not yet walk, talk or understand much of what was said to him.

My associate patted me on the shoulder. "It must be difficult," she said with an empathetic smile. "But you know, this will no doubt pull your family closer together."

It was such an innocuous statement and was said with such assurance that it took nearly an hour for me to really get mad. But it was a few days later when she told me that 'God never gives you more than you can stand," that I really got angry.

Did she think this tragedy was a test? Was I trying out for sainthood? Any God who would do this to a family was no friend of mine, I thought, and I've already got more than I can stand!

At the time I was trying to manage a newspaper, taking a few minutes from my desk to run to the hospital, sometimes as many as five times during the day. My children were being bounced from one relative to the other until I could get home, and then bounced back again while I rushed back to the hospital to visit their father. We lived on fast-food hamburgers and frozen pizza.

After the kids were tucked into bed, I wrote my stories for the newspaper or read or tried to figure out what was happening to our finances. I crawled into bed at midnight and was up at five in a fruitless effort to be organized for the day. The kids' homework suffered, and we were all tired and cranky.

Those were the easy times. From there it went downhill. As I struggled with problems, I kept hearing my associate's words, "this will pull your family closer together."

Somehow a statement said with such confidence tends to sit at the back of your mind and tickle your consciousness. Perhaps, if I were handling all this better, the family would be getting closer instead of falling apart, you think as you lay awake in the middle of the night. You look for a purpose. You look for any positive aspect of this tragedy, and when you can't find it, you wonder if you're just a bad person. Those few words, well-meaning as they were intended, can trigger a whole new layer of guilt and anger to add stress to your life.

And you don't need any more stress.

Let's say we took a large piece of a puzzle away and change its shape. That's essentially what happens when a family member is head-injured. We can wiggle that puzzle piece or turn it all directions, and it isn't going to fit into the puzzle the way it did before. In order for the puzzle to work when we put that piece back, the other pieces will have to change shapes too.

That's what happens when the brain-injured member comes back into the family. Each family member goes through role changes to adapt to the new circumstances. We may think that we've adapted to that person while he's been at the hospital. Maybe we've spent several hours there each day, helping with therapy, helping with meals or with dressing. We may have even developed whole new schedules and activities around that person. It's definitely a step in the right direction. That's not the same as living with him.

It may sound cruel, but while our family member was in the hospital, he was an activity for us. We went to visit. We helped the nurses. Then we went home and resumed the other parts of our lives, knowing that he was safe and well cared for.

And while he was in the hospital, we may have worried and suffered a great deal from stress, but we were free from the everyday problems of getting him to brush his teeth, of making sure he could get to the bathroom, of being embarrassed when he made rude remarks. We could still pretend that he was the same person we loved before.

It's much more difficult to ignore the changes, particularly behavior changes, when that person lives in our home. I find it difficult to watch the damage that has accrued over several years to our home as Dale spills, drops or scratches the fragile things, or trips over the furniture. But those problems are simple when compared to the damage that accrues to family members who don't know how to cope with this new person who may not be anywhere near as lovable as the person they knew before.

A family is a system with its own routines, laws, rhythms and internal communications. Each member of a family has a role to play, and that role in turn affects every other member's role. The normal family, if there is such a thing, runs along smoothly, everyone playing his own role and adjusting to the little changes in everyone else's role. But when one family member throws a giant wrench into the working parts of the family, roles begin to collide and gears grind because major adjustments simply can't be made quickly.

Depending on where the family relationships were when the brain injury occurred, families react in a variety of ways. Very often, in the beginning, the family does band together to try to help each other through the worst of the crisis. But there is no ritual which can put the disaster behind us as a funeral does when there is a death in the family. A head injury stays with you, continuing to burden the family with stress. There is no relief brought by full recovery as there might be after internal injuries. Prolonged stress begins to take a heavy toll on members of the family.

Families with these problems all seem to react in similar ways. A brain-injured person's family tries out a variety of ways to deal with the stress they are feeling, searching for a way to ease their pain. The grief process is only one of those coping mechanisms. Even after the family has accepted the loss of a family member as they once knew him, each family member must then live with this stranger. Many families eventually throw in the towel, unable to deal in healthy ways with the head-injured family member or with the rest of the family either.

It is particularly difficult for children to deal with this new family member. After all, this parent or child or sibling has been very ill. Children may remember a time when they got mad at this person and wished that he or she would die. They may already be consumed with guilt, thinking that what they wished when they were angry has nearly come true. They may go through the kind of process that another child I know—a boy named Andy—did.

Andy's father was brain-injured in an accident. At first, everything around him was total confusion. Mom went to the hospital and Andy went to Grandma's house. Grandma was especially solicitous, fixing him a special dessert and talking to him about how hard the doctors were working to help his dad. She had him sit with her as she said a long prayer asking God to help the doctors save his father's life. He could barely choke down his food, but Grandma hovered over him encouraging him to eat.

Mom finally came home from the hospital and picked him up from the couch where he'd been asleep and carried him out into the cold night to the car. He remembered his mother and grandmother whispering, but he was very sleepy. He asked his mother if his father was all right, and she nodded. When they got home, Mom tucked him into his bed, and he could hear her getting ready for bed. But several times during the night, he heard her get up out of bed and call the hospital.

The next morning she got him up and ready for school, but when he talked to her, she didn't seem to hear him. He noticed that she didn't eat her own breakfast, and it took her 15 minutes to find the car keys in plain sight on the kitchen counter. All day during school, he wondered if his dad was still alive. It was nearly impossible to concentrate on his work, and his teacher finally got so frustrated that she made him stay in during recess to finish his work. Neither Andy nor his mother, nor his grandmother thought to tell his teacher what had happened at home. Andy didn't know why he couldn't concentrate, but whenever he would try to do his math, he would think about his father. Andy and his father had many disagreements, and the boy had sometimes wished his father would disappear.

After school, Grandma picked Andy up, telling him that his mother would be going to the hospital after work and he would stay with Grandma again until she came to get him. Andy thought his grandmother seemed flustered, and they almost had a wreck on the way home. He had wanted to ask her how his dad was doing, but he decided to wait up to ask his mother since Grandma was so upset. By the time his mom got there, he was asleep on the couch again.

This went on, with variations, for several weeks. When Andy asked his mom how his dad was doing, she always said he was doing better. Finally she took him to the hospital to see his dad. Andy was looking forward to seeing him and was excited. He planned to hug his dad and tell him he loved him and that he didn't want him to go away. But when he walked into the hospital room, he didn't even recognize the person in the bed for several seconds. Andy was shocked to see that his dad's face was swollen like a cantaloupe on one side, and there was a big ugly red line with black stitches running across one side of his head. His mom told him to be careful when he touched his father so that he didn't hurt him. He couldn't bring himself to try and hug his dad and retreated to the other side of the room. A nurse came in and talked to Andy for a minute before she gave his dad a shot. The nurse talked very loudly and slowly to his dad, and he grunted at her but no one seemed to understand what he was trying to say.

Andy stood across the room and felt sick. He just wanted to go home. He was overwhelmed with guilt thinking about what his wish had done.

Over the ensuing weeks, his dad got better and came home. He couldn't keep his balance, couldn't speak well and couldn't remember things that happened only a few minutes earlier. He was angry at times and since he couldn't say what he wanted, he would often grab Andy and point him at something he wanted. If Andy still didn't understand, his father would grab his head and push the boy's face onto what he wanted.

Andy avoided his father whenever possible because he never knew when one of these episodes would erupt. When he complained to his mother, she said his dad couldn't help it and asked him to try harder to understand and be helpful. He knew that his father did the same things to his mother and even twisted her arm or hit her when she didn't understand what he wanted. Many times he heard his mother crying in the bathroom.

Even when his father got better, Andy could never tell when his dad would get frustrated and angry about something and start throwing things. Once Andy found one of his favorite shirts had been torn and thrown outside. He was very angry when he found the shirt and he confronted his father about it. His father said he hadn't done anything to the shirt and called Andy a dirty name. Andy screamed back that he hated him. His mom quieted his dad by turning on the television and told Andy she would get him a new shirt. He heard her crying later as she was fixing supper. He felt bad about the mess they were in but he hated the way his dad was now, and he hated the way his mother had to work all the time and never had time for anything but his dad. He decided he had to be the one who would help his mother.

He worked hard to become the family "hero," a role that many older children adopt during family crisis. He worked hard in school and made good grades; he helped around the house without being asked; he tried hard not to antagonize his dad. He was proud of the way his mother talked about him to other people, and told him how grown up he was. More and more, she asked his opinion about things that needed to be done around the house. When he got a job after school, the money helped with expenses. He won awards at school and was active in after school activities that kept him away from the house and his dad sitting in front of the television. Andy never missed a day of work.

But one day as he was sitting alone after school waiting for a friend, he realized that although he had made his mother proud and he had gotten awards and pats on the back, nothing had changed at home. His mother was still frazzled and emotional and his father was still irrational and unpredictable. Six years of therapy didn't seem to have made any difference at all. And his mom had told him that she didn't think they could afford to send him to college, even with his good grades and awards. He would have to work to help out. What was the use of the work he had done? He was still in the same place he had started—hating his dad and afraid for his mom.

Slowly, Andy began to give up. He quit studying. His grades fell and he became moody and disruptive in class, insulting his teachers and shutting out his friends. He felt that nobody really cared about his problems. They thought that he was like everyone else but they didn't really know how bad it was at his house—how crazy it was. So he spent more time with Jack, a fellow whose father drank a lot and beat Jack up. Jack and he understood each other. They tried marijuana together. Andy began to be late to work, sometimes showing up stoned. He got fired.

His mom, who had been worried about him and who had learned to count on Andy's income, berated Andy and told him that he had let her down. She would have to find another job or something to make up for his lost job. Andy just stared at her and decided she didn't care about him either. Nothing he'd done for her mattered, only the money. Nothing would ever change at their house so he might as well leave. He dropped out of school, got a job, and he and Jack moved in together. It didn't last long and he had to move back in with his folks where the bickering got worse. He had their attention but this time it was all negative. He smoked more and locked himself in his room, avoiding them during the day and slipping out at night. He was no longer their hero and he was depressed and angry. Andy had fallen into the role known as "scapegoat."

Other roles are adopted in a dysfunctional family like Andy's. Most children try hard to band together in the first days and weeks of the crisis and work together. But when nothing seems to get better, and they stop seeing much progress in the head-injured person's recovery, they begin to fall apart. And unlike the families of alcoholics, families of brain-injured people have no clear focus for their anger. They believe they can't be angry at someone who's injured and not able to be rational, but they have nowhere to go with the anger that is there so it spews out on anyone who happens to be near. And hope for improvement dies after the family realizes that the brain-injured person is home to stay—just as he is.

The whole family feels trapped. If they withdraw from their loved one, they are abandoning an innocent person. They can't even talk about such a terrible thing. Yet the other possibility is so frightening they can't face it either. It seems to them that if they stay, they will be unhappy and unable to form a life away from this craziness. Around and around, like a puppy chasing its tail, their thought processes follow these two possibilities. They feel like prisoners, but to escape would be treason. And they feel very guilty about the way they feel.

Heroes and scapegoats are common in such families. If mom is being the hero, there is little room for big sister to adopt the role. If dad is a scapegoat, drinking and being demanding, there may not be room for another one. But none of them are operating alone. Other family members are dealing with their feelings in different ways.

Some are deniers, becoming withdrawn and doing their best to ignore the whole situation. They don't draw attention to themselves, and if something comes up, they simply go away, often disappearing into their rooms to read. They are like robots, never disagreeing or agreeing, simply getting through what needs to be done and then disappearing into their own worlds again.

Another child might try to erase everyone's pain by being the most helpful child ever born. She'll bake cookies, sew on buttons or comb someone's hair. She'll listen to Mom's problems, rub her back and make dinner so she can rest. She'll tell jokes and be a clown to make people laugh. She is the nurturer, always helping someone else, often at the expense of her own psyche. She may even become the focal point of the whole family, because, without her, things would be too difficult and painful to bear, and the family might fall apart. This person can be either a child or an adult. Often it is the oldest female child or mom.

Interestingly enough, with all the pain that's going on in such a family, no one talks about the real problem. That problem is how to deal with our head-injured family member so that we can also enjoy life. But family members are most likely saying to themselves, "This person is making my life miserable, and I know no way to make it smoother other than to leave. And I could never leave." Guilt lays heavily over such a family. Each family member may believe he or she is the only one having such terrible thoughts. They feel guilty for not being more altruistic, and since they don't want other members of the family to find out how terrible they are, they never mention that they feel trapped. So each one is going around in his or her lonely little world, feeling angry and feeling guilty.

Presto. Depression is just around the corner.

A depressed family is an accident waiting to happen. Some family members will literally become accident prone—falling down stairs, stepping out in front of a car, driving carelessly. It's a half-hearted attempt at suicide.

106

Other family members may actually feel so helpless and guilty that they will seriously consider suicide. Some will begin to drink or use drugs to dull their feelings of hopelessness, or anger or guilt.

A family member may worry incessantly about what is going on in his own family or even in the world. He may accept the blame for the head injury, the family's financial problems, corruption in politics and—well why not—the atom bomb.

Beth was like that. She found herself worrying about everything. Some of the worries were logical because they were very real problems. She was having financial difficulties now that her husband was disabled. She was concerned about her children who seemed to be running with a bad crowd. But she also worried about whether or not there would be a nuclear war, and she thought a great deal about what sins she had committed in her lifetime. She was becoming more and more fanatical in her religion and became convinced that her children would go to hell if she couldn't get them to church more often. The harder she pushed them, the more adamantly they refused. She was such a terrible mother, she decided, she didn't even deserve to have children. She had failed them.

The more Beth worried about the children's spirituality and her own financial future, the less she was able to sleep. She found herself getting up at 2 a.m. and eating a bowl of cereal to calm her nerves. She gained weight. When she got up in the morning, she looked in the mirror and shrugged. What did it matter that she no longer bothered with makeup or her hair. She knew her husband didn't notice. He was much too absorbed in his own struggle. They rarely talked. She just took care of his physical needs.

She felt exhausted and unable to summon energy for the smallest jobs. When the children had to fix their own meals or wash their own clothes, she felt guilty. They must hate her, she thought.

She never felt happy anymore. Sometimes when they were watching television, the rest of the family would laugh at something and she would wonder what they found so funny. Mostly she wanted to just feel alive again. But there didn't seem to be any hope of that, and she didn't deserve it anyway. She wished she could lie down on the bed and drift into a sleep that would last forever. If she were dead, no one would notice that she was gone.

Beth was caught up in a depression that would have consumed her if she hadn't finally talked to her doctor about how badly she felt. He sent her to a therapist who was knowledgeable about dysfunctional families. The therapist helped her separate her very real problems and priorities from those she couldn't control. He also convinced her that in order for her to help to family, she needed to have something good in her own life.

While depression is the most serious immediate concern in a family dealing with brain injury, other problems may appear over time. If children adopt the hero role and spend their time trying to live up to impossible expectations during their school years, they may go on to develop unhealthy, compulsively perfectionist personalities, never being able to live up to their own expectations.

Deniers may never be able to form relationships, since they never emerged from their own worlds long enough to do so. They continue to withdraw from problems and from other people, living empty and lonely lives.

Pain erasers may continue their selfless activities into their adulthood, always forming a relationship in which the other person is dependent on the nurturing function that this person provides. Eventually, that nurturing may give way to resentment as the pain eraser wonders when someone is going to erase his pain.

But there is good news. Families don't have to fall into these patterns. There are ways of avoiding the pitfalls. Education is one way, so read up on dysfunctional families or talk to school counselors or others with experience in this area. Most importantly, accept your emotions as normal and talk with your family about them. Many families have been able to work out solutions to the embarrassing or frightening situations they find themselves dealing with just by admitting their concerns to each other and working together to bring change.

When Dale was unpredictable and occasionally threatening toward the kids, I was able to act as a go-between and a referee. As an adult, I was better able to handle his outbursts and to act with authority than were the kids. We talked about our problems and tried to find creative solutions. Many times we succeeded. And when things got too difficult for us to resolve alone, we consulted a counselor.

It's usually easier to ask for help for the brain-injured member of your family than it is to ask for help for the rest of the family. After all, that person is the one who's sick. But, because no one operates in a vacuum, the brain-injured person is not the only person in the family that may need help adjusting to a new role.

Having a trusted friend to talk to, one who won't judge you for thinking terrible thoughts, is a great help. But if you feel that you're becoming overwhelmed with problems and worries, if you can't get interested in the things you've loved before, if you've lost your sense of humor, if your sleep patterns are awry, and you can't see any way out of the difficult emotional pit you find yourself in, it's time to ask for professional help. Emotional problems often lead to physical problems as well. Ask yourself what would happen if the whole family got sick. That would be measurably worse than swallowing some pride and calling a counselor for help.

Ten Difficult Issues You May Have to Deal With

1.Guilt when you have contributed to the brain injury in some way.

2. Deep depression, often accompanied by chemical crutches, when life seems without meaning.

3.Anger, also associated with drugs or alcohol, which is expressed in violence toward yourself or others.

4. Loss of an intimate relationship, whether with the brain-injured person or with other members of your family who don't seem to have time for you.

5. Guilt when you don't feel the same about the brain-injured person and no longer want to spend your life with him or her.

6. A belief that a brain-injured person cannot be as good or as happy as before unless he/she recovers completely.

7. Abandonment by friends and family.

8. Feeling trapped.

9. Feeling that you have no economic or emotional control over your life.

10. Feeling that no one understands what you are going through. (I do.)

Taking Control

When Dale and I went in to apply for Social Security disability benefits, we first made an appointment with one of the office's representatives. I was extremely uncomfortable with the whole idea of applying for Social Security Disability, since it seemed very much like accepting charity to me, and I fidgeted while we waited in the outer office. After a half hour of waiting, we were called back to a desk where a woman sat working at her computer. As we approached, she looked up and then motioned us toward the two chairs in front of her desk. Without looking at either of us, she took the papers we offered and sat silently perusing them. Finally, again without looking at us, she tapped at her computer for a few minutes, she asked a couple of questions, and then got up from her desk and walked away.

I watched as she stopped at several desks to chat with other women. Finally at the far end of the room, she halted in front of a copy machine and made copies of our documents. While the copy machine was running she fiddled with her hair and called across the room to ask someone about his weekend. When she returned, she dropped our papers on the desk in front of us, told us it would be a few weeks before we heard from Social Security and dismissed us. Not once had she addressed us by name or looked at our faces. I felt as if we were dirt that had just been swept under her rug.

As we walked out of the office, I was so furious that I couldn't even answer Dale when he asked what was wrong with me. If I had been alone, I would have rushed to my car and cried. As it was, I swallowed the tears and fumed. Now I know I should have been more assertive with the woman, asked more questions and if she had still treated us shabbily I could have asked for a supervisor. But at the time, already feeling slightly unworthy because we were asking for help, I did nothing except let my stomach tie up in knots and miss yet another night's sleep.

Too many of us feel the way I did that day. We are already beaten down by tragedy. Our lives are in chaos, and we are confronted with a whole new reality. We tend to withdraw and let others control our lives. But when we do that, we lose more and more control over our own lives. And that means we also lose confidence and our sense of dignity, ending up in a very stressful situation. Don't we already have enough problems?

We have to become aggressive questioners and aggressive demanders. We need to control as many facets of our lives as we can. The comfort that comes from knowing where the next problem may crop up is lifesaving. There is nothing worse than the wordless fear that exists inside when you feel your life is out of control.

Knowledge: The Heavy Duty Shock Absorber

Imagine that I sent you to the grocery store with a grocery list like this:

Beans

cheese

meat

oil

bread

Since you have no idea what I'm planning for dinner or what brands I usually buy, you might have a little difficulty with this list. But if you know that I want green beans, mozzarella cheese, Italian sausage, motor oil and wheat bread, you might find shopping a little less stressful. (And the car won't seize up either.) Better yet, if you know which brands and how much I wanted of each item, you would have no problems at all with the shopping. The more knowledge you have, the easier your decisions become.

It's the same with brain-injury. No, I'm not saying you must go out and train as a brain surgeon, but I do believe you should learn everything you can about the brain. You should ask questions continually. Why does the doctor believe there is a reason to expect hearing loss? Why are the therapists practicing rhythm games with your brain-injured family member? What is the next step in therapy?

Read until your eyes feel like they're going to fall out. Every little piece of information will help you to understand what health professionals are saying and will enable you to ask even more questions. Keep asking even if people are annoyed by your questions.

Never let yourself be intimidated by professional jargon. If you don't understand a doctor's explanation, ask him or her to explain a different way. It used to be easy for doctors to tell us what was best for us and for us to accept that as gospel. But as we learn more, we realize that doctors, therapists and other professionals are just people. They make mistakes. They err in judgment. And sometimes they may even be jerks.

One family whose son was gravely injured in an auto accident found it impossible to speak with the neurosurgeon who was treating the boy. They waited in his room. They called the surgeon's office. They asked the nurses to have him call them. But the surgeon ignored them. It took threats of a lawsuit and a letter to the medical review board before the surgeon would sit down with them (two weeks later) and tell them what was happening with their son.

This surgeon's behavior in this case was inexcusable. Although he was giving the patient the best of care, he was neglecting the family. Perhaps he didn't realize that families are units. This family was convinced the surgeon thought they were too dumb to understand anything. Whether or not they could understand all the complexities is beside the point. They deserved to hear what was happening to their son directly from the doctor who was treating him.

Most physicians don't act so insensitively. But even if they do, their mistakes won't have as much impact if we have enough knowledge to recognize those mistakes for what they are. There are many stories among head injury families about doctors who expressed doubt that an injured person would ever be able to function again, when subsequently that person has made a remarkable recovery. Although we tend to blame physicians as unfeeling, we forget that their experience has probably made them wary of expecting recovery. There are doctors who should not be excused for the truly stupid errors they make, but we also need to understand the problems of physicians who deal with head injury. Their whole lives are surrounded by the tragedies of families like ours. They see more failure than success, and yet they are expected to go on digging around in people's brains in hope of saving another life.

Therapists, too, are confronted every day with failure. Even the most caring people can become burned out under the circumstances of head injury. It is much easier for those people to expect failure and be surprised with success than to expect success and be beaten down by failure. They cannot allow themselves the emotional investment with each patient that we, as family members, expect. Our brain-injured family member is one of many such tragedies to the professionals. They, too, face a continual barrage of pain.

It's very easy for us to turn our anger against the medical professionals who treat our family member because they aren't trying hard enough or don't give enough or don't expect to succeed. But they're only people who have a limited amount of energy to give. We have to keep our perspective.

But that doesn't mean you can't ask questions and expect to get information. I'll admit that some professionals are threatened by assertive family members. But the best of them expect and appreciate the family's total involvement because they know that their patient will make the best improvement if the family approaches the injury with as much caring and knowledge as possible.

As you read about head injury, about the brain, about therapy, you may decide to ask for second opinions. If you've had a good relationship with your current doctor or hospital, they may be offended when you tell them that's what you're going to do. It's only natural for them to feel like you're questioning their abilities but they do understand the need for second opinions, and you shouldn't be intimidated by their defensiveness. Remember that treatment methods for brain injury are undergoing enormous change. Technology and research are making giant strides forward in helping brain-injured people recover. No single health professional can know everything there is to know about head injury. Things are changing too fast for anyone to keep up.

Your responsibility is to your brain-injured family member. Ironically, a year after Dale's surgery, a new technique was developed which, had it been available earlier, might possibly have prevented his disability. Of course, had we waited for that development, he most likely would have died. Had we known it was under development would we have made different choices? Would the surgeon have suggested different alternatives?

If you are satisfied that you have researched the possible alternatives, questions like these won't bother you very much. So ask questions. Research as much as you can. The Internet (start with www.medline.org) and your local library can provide you with an enormous amount of good information, and second opinions can give you a different viewpoint. The list of books written for those of us who aren't medical professionals grows longer every year. The National Head Injury Foundation and the National Brain Injury Foundation maintain reading lists, and Amazon.com and other on-line bookstores will allow you to search out hundreds of resources in a short time. I urge you to contact your state foundation for recommendations as well as a list of local support groups who can help you as well. The national foundations are listed in the back of this book along with phone numbers and web addresses for your quick reference.

Being Assertive

The most powerless people in the world are those who don't know how to get the information they need and are afraid to ask. You don't need to be without the power that information can give you.

Ask questions! Too many times a family will be denied aid simply because they don't realize that there are other avenues to reach the same objective. One family's insurance company won't pay for a private nurse to accompany their child to school. But if they call the trip to school an "educational outing" the company will pay. So every trip to school is an educational outing. Silly? Yes, but sometimes you just have to play the game by the system's rules.

I was stunned when we got a denial of Social Security benefits after our first application. When we received the official notice, Dale was sleeping most of the day or watching television. He couldn't speak, read, get around well, remember how to turn on the stove or even remember our names.

The notice said he was not disabled because he did not need a cane to walk.

I can still imagine the clerk who made that determination going through his/her list of reasons to deny the claim and saying, "Oh, I haven't used this one for a while—I'll just say 'denied for no cane.'" Most of us who've been through the system now know that you'd have to be dead to have a claim accepted the first time it's filed with Social Security. Don't accept this ploy if you know they're wrong. Turn it around and file an appeal.

I'm sure I went into a mild shock, fearing that we would lose our home, fearing that I wouldn't be able to feed the kids, fearing—yikes—fearing everything! I hardly read the fine print that said we could appeal the decision. The very nice man at the Social Security office who I talked with gently told me to appeal and the claim would no doubt be approved. And it was, six months later.

I worry about the people who don't get that message and who give up. The system is often cruel and unfeeling. There is too much paper work during a time when our minds are slightly addled by crisis. The rules are often nonsensical to us, and the forms are complicated and full of jargon. The people are difficult to work with sometimes and treat us as if we're bothering them. Although we can work to change that over time, for now, we just have to play by their rules.

I find it helps for me to build up a reserve of anger before I deal with "the system." That slow burn gives me a little extra energy and aggressiveness which allows me to demand answers and ask for more than a particular company or agency routinely gives out. To do that, I just replay my little mental tape of all the rudeness and injustice I've had to go through. I'm not all smiles when I go in, but I come out feeling much better -- usually.

Many times a case manager will have been assigned to you at the hospital. By all means use that service. A case manager, usually a specially trained social worker, can help to coordinate care and rehabilitation systems, work with insurance companies, find services and resources and work as a go-between for the family and the confusing and complex maze of agencies. Some organizations like Catholic Charities, Jewish American Services Associations, and local religious organizations may provide case management free of charge. Rehabilitation hospitals often help you find a case manager if they don't have them on staff. If you haven't been able to obtain the aid you are entitled to by yourself or with the help of a case manager, you may want to discuss your options with a lawyer. Although I believe that legal action is sometimes much more stressful and certainly more expensive than dealing with the details of insurance and other resources, it is sometimes necessary to rely on a legal expert. Many lawyers will take your financial circumstances into account when determining your fee, but be aware that some people will also try to take advantage of your situation to line their own pockets. Once again, the more you know, the better off you will be. Ask your local support group if they can recommend a lawyer who is experienced in dealing with brain injury. Talk to several lawyers and try to determine if you and the lawyer have the same principles and goals. Then discuss fees. Most practicing attorneys are willing to spend a little time with you at little or no charge to get to know you and explain their philosophy. Just don't expect to get free legal advice.

I feel badly that we must sometimes resort to demands and legal battles to get the best help for our family. In a perfect world everyone would be fair, but this world is far from perfect and you have to be assertive in response. For those of us who were taught to always be nice and polite, this is not an easy adjustment.

Just remember that you have a family to consider; a family that is already under attack from every direction needs to become its own little army. Luckily, you have lots of friends to help you defend your family. You just need to know that they are there.

Ask questions. Read. Surf the web. Knowledge is power.

Ideas you need to acknowledge as unrealistic

1. Someone is going to come along and rescue you from this.

2. If you just cling to your familiar routine, in time things will get back to normal.

3. You can control things well enough to keep the healthy members of your family from being affected by the head injury.

4. Medical professionals will make all the right decisions for you.

5. Your brain-injured family member will eventually be just the same as before.

6. Your friends will all understand your pain and be there for you with extra support throughout the recovery period.

7. People will treat you with more kindness and consideration because they know you're under more than usual stress.

8. Your family members will all work together for the brain-injured person's recovery and you'll all be drawn closer by this crisis.

9. You will be "just fine" without help from anyone because you are tough.

Detaching

After 17 years of working hard to blend my life and Dale's life into a compatible mix, learning to step back and detach myself from his problems was one of the most difficult and one of the most important tasks I've ever attempted. In college I typed his papers and worked to support us. When he went to work as an engineer, I made sure that his wardrobe matched his promotions and I entertained his colleagues. I edited his written presentations and made suggestions when he asked my opinion. We worked together to make the kids' experience with 4-H a positive one. When he was a Cub Scout leader, I was always there with cookies and milk.

To step back and give up the role of constant backup seemed like abandonment to me. All my life I had been listening to my family's and society's criticism of family members who didn't support their own. How many times had I heard that a man's success was foiled by his wife's lack of help and support? That a child would have made something of himself except his parents weren't there when he needed them? I KNEW what was expected of me when Dale was brain-injured. I would stand by him. I would take care of him. And I would do it better than anyone else in the world.

But I had no idea of what that kind of involvement meant— to Dale, to me and to our children. And it very nearly destroyed us all.

Each of us has a limit to our time, abilities, energies, and most of all, to the control we can exercise over others. I approached this task of supporting Dale as if those limits didn't apply to me. I invested everything in helping him, at the expense of my health, my ego, my mental stability and my children's environment. I thought if I was just strong enough and helpful enough, everything would be fine again.

I was wrong.

When I sat down and worked with Dale on his therapy as his therapist wanted, I had no time to help the kids with their homework. When Dale needed transportation or help with a problem, I took time from work and then was appalled when the lack of preparation time showed up in something I had written. If I spent time with the children, Dale felt left out, and I felt guilty for not giving him enough. If I didn't take time with the children, I felt guilty because they weren't getting enough support. When I was frustrated at Dale's lack of motivation, I would yell at Mike or Kara. I simply couldn't balance all the demands and felt very much a failure. Somehow, I was to blame for everything.

One particularly bad day, a few months after Dale's brain injury, I was rushing around the kitchen throwing together a casserole for dinner. It had been a long, difficult day at work, and when I walked into the house, the family began listing their needs for the evening. Kara needed a costume for a school play. Mike needed new gym shoes. Dale was supposed to read a paragraph while I timed it several consecutive times. They were all hungry.

As I worked in the kitchen, I tried to figure out a schedule in which all those needs could be included. I would be sewing the costume late into the night, and I had an early breakfast meeting the next morning. I had to get all those problems worked out somehow.

One by one the family filed into the kitchen to ask what was for supper. When I told them, everyone turned up their noses.

128

Kara didn't like the mushrooms that I'd put in the casserole. Mike complained that we had to eat that particular casserole ALL the time. Dale simply announced that he wasn't going to eat it. With each complaint I grew more frustrated and angry. This casserole had been eaten with gusto by the whole family only two weeks before. What did they expect of me anyway?

As I seethed, trying not to snap back, poor Mike had one last comment that cut to the bone. "John's mom never makes him eat stuff like this." It was the last straw.

I lost every last bit of control. I swung around and, screaming at the top of my voice, I beat both fists against the overhead vent above the stove. Bang! Bang! Bang!

CRASH! The vent tore loose from the wall and fell onto the stove, breaking the glass casserole dish that I had just taken from the oven. The dish shattered and glass, hot noodles, mushrooms and cheese flew all over the kitchen.

I stood looking at the mess and began to cry. The children, frightened and sobbing hysterically, grabbed me around the waist. Mike, thinking that it was all his fault, sobbed his apologies over and over again. Dale swore and stormed out of the kitchen.

That was the point to which all of my, and society's, expectations had brought us. We were in trouble. I simply could not do what was expected, and I couldn't control what was happening to my family.

I thought I should be able to control the amount of pain they felt. I thought I should be able to control how they acted. I thought I should be able to control what people thought about us. I set myself up for failure and then blamed myself for failing.

Nobody could have done all that, even if they weren't under tremendous stress.

No one knows, until they have lived it, the kind of stress that brain injury places on families. They only see what is apparent—that a family member has been hurt. That's where their understanding stops and judgments begin. And if family members aren't already struggling with pervasive guilt, the expectations of society will certainly bring on a serious case of self-punishment.

It's possible to deal with this judgment if you can detach yourself from both your own expectations and the expectations of your neighbors and society as a whole. It takes hard work and a thick skin. You have to learn to weigh the needs of those people directly involved and ignore the judgments of those who don't understand. In a world where we've learned to judge our behavior patterns by being judged, that's a monumental task. But the relief it provides is also monumental.

Detachment is a two-fold process. First comes the business of learning not to feel intimidated or pressured by people who are not involved. That often comes from anger, and it's easier to arrive at than the second kind of detachment. That second, very important kind of detachment involves freeing yourself from your own unreasonable expectations and it is very, very difficult.

Other people react strangely to brain injury. One family tells of a neighbor who was extremely helpful and solicitous while their head-injured son was in the hospital, but who avoided them after he was home. "It was as if she thought he was contagious," they said. They can laugh about it now that a few years have passed, but at the time, it hurt.

People sometimes think that because they aren't as emotionally involved as you are, they have the simple answer that you need. "You should have asked about this," they'll say, or "You should have done that." Maybe they'll be bold enough to tell you that if you had been more thoughtful (brave, gentle, intelligent, caring…) you would have done such-and-such. "Can't you do what I did?" is a good one. They all mean well, I think. And it's easy for people to make judgments when they aren't actively involved in the situation. The answers look easy from their perspective.

Learn to say, "Hmm. I'll consider that," if you feel the need. But realize that to yourself you should be saying: "They don't know what they're talking about, but THAT is not my problem."

It's not my problem if a therapist believes I'm shirking my responsibilities when I choose to take in Mike's concert instead of helping Dale with his therapy. It's not my problem that people stare at us when Dale is having difficulty talking to a store clerk. It's not my problem that some of our friends have drifted away. I can't control what other people believe about me or what actions they take. All I can control is my response.

And I know what I have chosen to do or say was chosen with regard to my own personal situation. I weighed the alternatives. I know what my resources are and what the needs of my family include, and I make choices based only on those alternatives— not on what other people think I should do.

Maybe I'm lucky that I was born pigheaded and raised to be independent. I have learned not to care about the judgments that other people place on me because I can only deal with my problems. What they believe about me is not my problem. What they believe about Dale or my children is not my problem. I simply don't have the time or the energy to deal with something that I can't change. I can only take responsibility for those things that I have some measure of control over. I've had to take a step back from the hurt and pain of other people's judgment to where I can get a better view.

Detaching myself from my OWN expectations, however, was much more difficult. All of my self-esteem was wrapped up in what I believed I could control in my life. I thought I could control how the children felt about their father and how he behaved. I thought I could control how other people reacted to Dale's disability. If I had a dollar for every time I have tried to change someone's belief about brain injury, I'd be rich! What a shock to my ego it was to find that I couldn't control any of that. I couldn't even control the way I felt.

I'd like to believe that I'm really and truly a "good" person. But when I get resentful that I have to explain a simple idea to Dale several different ways before he understands it, I lose that concept of myself. I SHOULD be more understanding. I SHOULD be more patient. I have a list of shoulds that would stretch miles, and I don't live up to many of them on a regular basis. And until I learned to quit judging myself against these impossible standards, I heaped guilt and anger on myself until I was almost buried.

I finally gave myself a break. Nope, I'm not perfect, and I don't always do what I SHOULD. But for the most part, I try to do what I can to help Dale with his problems and to raise my children with love and understanding.

I allow myself to think really bad things because I know that they are only emotions to which I have a legitimate right. I say what I think, even though it sometimes offends people. I don't allow people to make me feel guilty, and I'm not going to let ME make me feel guilty. Or at least I'm working on it.
132

Dale went through a period of accusing me of sleeping around with his friends and anyone else who might occur to him. It nearly drove me crazy because I couldn't understand why he thought that. After all, I was either working or taking care of him. How could I even have TIME for sleeping around? (Even if I wanted to and had found time for that kind of thing, or had found anyone who would be interested in a tired, haggard-looking woman, I would probably have fallen asleep before anything happened.) I spent a lot of time trying to reason with him, even though he was pretty incapable of reasoning at the time.

Finally it dawned on me. It wasn't my problem. I was doing nothing wrong. If he wanted to believe that I was sleeping around, even after all evidence to the contrary was presented, there was nothing I could do about it. So I stopped worrying about it and ignored his accusations. As soon as I stopped letting it be my problem, the accusations slowly disappeared. Because I thought it was a problem for me to solve, Dale was able to control me with his accusations. That's what had kept the conflict alive. It was one way for him to once again be able to control someone. He was striking out against his injury and searching for someone to punish for it. I let myself be drawn into that because I let him make me feel like it was my problem. It wasn't.

If we take other people's judgments to heart and if we torture ourselves with our own judgments, we become little more than puppets—controlled by everyone else and unable to live a peaceful life.

No matter how much you love your head-injured family member, you must learn to detach your expectations and those of the rest of society from your own personal worth. If you stake your own sense of well-being on how your head-injured loved one recovers or behaves, or how other people behave, you're in for a long, rocky fall.

Each of us has a life to live, and we deserve to enjoy it. If you are letting brain injury make your life miserable, you are probably threatening your physical health as well. Make sure your brain-injured family member is safe and doesn't threaten anyone else, but don't let his or her lack of social grace keep you from living a full and joyful life yourself. You won't change anything by being miserable. Learn to give yourself a break. You can't solve all the problems because all the problems aren't yours to solve.

I think of detachment as the process of closing off just a little piece of my heart and my mind. Oh, how difficult it was to close the door against all that emotion and all those "shoulds." I had to give up a lot of my feelings of control by putting them on the other side of the door. But the end result has been more real control over my own life and a great deal more peace.

A few months ago, Mike gave me a little psychic gift. "You know, Mom," he said, "at first you used to be pretty hard on us about the way we felt about Dad. But when you lightened up and quit trying to make us understand, life was a lot easier. And I like Dad better now too."

Special Problems

Spouses

In sickness and health. Yup, that's what I vowed during the wedding ceremony. Nobody told me about brain injury. I thought of sickness as the flu—maybe pneumonia. Maybe there were cases of spouses who died of cancer, but that wouldn't happen to us. I was expecting health when I got married at 19. Everybody I knew was healthy.

Dale's brain injury changed all that. He was 38 when this started. Our relationship was good at times and stormy at others, but at least we knew pretty much where we stood with each other. I took care of the kids and the house—those were my major responsibilities. He took care of the car, doing repairs around the house, earning a good wage, and controlling our budget. While I often rebelled against his decisions, he was a strong force in the way we lived. In many ways, he controlled our lives. When he was disabled, our family roles began to flip-flop.

Let's take, for example, the garage door. Before Dale's surgery, we had bought a new wooden "people" door for our garage. The old one was warped and splintered, and we hadn't gotten a new one up before the surgery. For a year afterward, the new door stood silently, reproachfully, in the garage as the old one fell apart and finally even allowed small snow drifts to form on the garage floor. Trying to be sensitive, I asked Dale time and time again if we could have a friend help us hang the door.

"No!" he roared. "I will do it myself!"

Because I didn't want to hurt his feelings, I waited. Finally, furious that we were allowing the house to fall apart and opportunistic stray cats to take up residence behind the freezer in the garage, I decided to hang the door myself. I hadn't had much training except growing up on the ranch but I knew how to use a wood chisel and a hammer and screwdriver. Mike was willing to help. It took us all day long to get the door up and, to be honest, it didn't approach the quality of work that Dale expected. He had nothing but insults for our efforts. We'd ruined the door as far as he was concerned and he barely spoke to us. But it kept the snow and cats out, and Mike and I were proud of ourselves for having completed this task successfully. We'd taken a step toward controlling our lives and had built our confidence in our ability to take on more.

The cost was high. As I took over more and more of the tasks Dale considered his own, he became morose and depressed. As I became more confident and more comfortable making decisions about everything, Dale felt useless and emasculated. Because he made unreasonable demands of the kids, they ignored his orders or suggestions. Because he could no longer help with their homework, they asked me. Although I realized that it was difficult for him, it was the only plausible way for the family to continue to operate. Somebody had to be in charge, and he wasn't capable.

I didn't really understand to what extent he was troubled by all these changes until I attended a therapy session with him during which a counselor asked him what a father was supposed to do. Tears ran down his cheeks as he pounded his fist on the table and struggled for words.

"A father controls the family," he finally managed in a strangled shout.

"Is that all a father does?" the therapist asked.

"Yes," he said. "The father tells what to do."

There was no mention of love or kindness. Only control.

I knew we were in for a long battle. And it was sometimes a physical battle where I was frightened to death of him.

He began to invent little games—like trying to keep me from entering or leaving a room. No amount of reasoning would convince him to let me pass—not something burning on the stove—not a ringing phone—nothing. When the children were small, they had sometimes played similar games with me as a way to keep my attention. But with them, it was fairly easy for me to pick them up and move them, give them a hug, and get on with whatever task was necessary. Moving a six-foot, 185-pound man is much more difficult. And painful.

He would try to trip me as I crossed the room. He would twist my arm if I didn't respond as quickly as he wanted or drag me across the room to make me aware of something he wanted. He would do the same with the kids. At first they saw it as a funny game that Dad was playing. But it soon became clear that they would be hurt if they didn't let him win.

It had to stop. And it came to a head one cold day as I was trying to bring a bag of groceries into the house. Dale wanted me to stay outside. I was cold and tired and I shouldered my way past him, set down the groceries and went back outside to the car for another bag. Dale rushed past me and wouldn't let me go to the car. I tried reasoning. He just laughed. I tried to go back inside, but he stopped me. Finally, he twisted my arm behind my back and was pushing me around the yard. I had had enough.

"If you don't stop, I'm going to call the police and have you arrested," I shouted.

He stopped, still holding my arm behind my back. "What?"

"You're hurting me. If you don't stop, I'll have you arrested."

His face went white and his mouth hung open as he realized that I was serious. He dropped my arm and looked at me. "You mean that!" he finally said incredulously. He couldn't believe that I had threatened him. It was the first time that he'd taken seriously an assertion of mine that he was doing something wrong.

The role reversal was pretty much complete at that point. Except for occasional attempts to control the kids, or occasional temper tantrums that we were mostly able to keep non-violent, Dale was a bit easier to live with. But his depression grew. At times I fully expected to arrive home and find that he had killed himself. I worried about the children coming home to such a scene while I was at work.

Since Dale had been an avid hunter, our house was full of guns. I carefully hid all the ammunition and covered the guns so the sight of them wouldn't spark an idea. His depression was as frightening as the earlier harassment.

Role reversals are difficult for everyone. But in a marriage, role reversals brought on so suddenly can place tremendous demands on everyone. Dale couldn't see that I was doing two jobs—two people's jobs. He only saw that I was doing HIS tasks and resented it. Even though he began to take over some jobs in the house, he didn't see that as important because his real work was done by me. His anger and resentment were often acted out. When he began doing much of the cooking, any attempt by another family member to go into the kitchen and cook something was met with deep resentment and constant criticism.

138

He criticized my money decisions. He found fault with the kids in whatever they did. Counseling helped and he eventually began to learn better ways of dealing with his anger, but the family paid dearly.

Spouses have to deal squarely with the resentment that head-injured people feel because they are the most obvious and first target for anger. Fear is a very real concern for many wives, and some husbands, who find no other way to deal with the loss of control than harassment and punishment.

You cannot live your life in fear. Counseling can help. Threatening punishment helped me. But sometimes it will be impossible to stop violence from being used as a way to control the spouse. You are not required to suffer physical and/or emotional punishment because you are married to someone who is brain-injured. Many people will stay with a spouse and suffer indescribable emotional and physical pain because they feel they can't escape. Yet if that spouse were not head-injured, these intelligent people would have left long before or found a way to stop the abuse. Don't let your own guilt or society's expectations kill you. If you can't find a way to stop the punishment, get out, or place your brain-injured spouse in a place where he or she can be cared for by others. You may feel trapped, but you don't have to be mired in a life of violence and abuse.

But, of course, threatening behavior is not the only problem for spouses. The loss of an intimate relationship is a very difficult problem to deal with. Brain injury can cause an inordinate desire for sex or a lack of interest in sex or intimacy of any kind. It doesn't really have much to do with the way a person was before, or whether desire for sexual activity is coupled with an inability to perform.

Because sexual attraction is so dependent on personality and/or physical beauty, a brain injury can have a devastating effect on a marriage. If your husband was once a kind, warm and considerate lover, you may not find him desirable now that he is demanding, aggressive and constantly making lewd advances or remarks to you in front of others. If your wife was warm and responsive before her brain injury, you may feel incomplete, lonely and frustrated now that she is cold and unemotional or now that she is childlike and scarred. Perhaps you are simply unable to feel desire for someone who is disabled, physically and/or intellectually. Many times a spouse may simply be too exhausted from the duties of caring for a family to be interested in intimacy.

In the 17 years that Dale and I were married before his brain injury, two of the most important ingredients in our continuing affections for each other were a strong and satisfying sexual relationship and an equally satisfying intellectual relationship.

His brain injury stole both from us. And more than the loss of income, of friends, of the future we had planned, that loss cut to the core of our marriage. Before this happened, if I was troubled by something, I could discuss it with Dale knowing that his insight could help me sort out the problem. I could count on a hug when I was down. I could share an interesting article from the newspaper or an anecdote from work. Even if we didn't agree on everything we talked about, I knew that he was there as a friend and as a lover.

But after the brain injury, I could count on none of that. The only thing I could count on for sure was Dale's incessant and uncontrolled desire for sex. There was no seduction involved. Any sign of tenderness, an embrace or a quick kiss on his cheek, would bring an instant arousal on his part and he would act on it.

Exhausted, worried and overworked, I found myself drawing away from him. I stopped, almost completely, any physical show of affection. I did not kiss or embrace him. I dressed in the bathroom to avoid his eyes. I carefully avoided his touch. Our lovemaking, if you could call it that, dwindled to nothing. Although he would occasionally ask why I didn't want to make love, I couldn't bring myself to tell him that I couldn't bear to have him touch me. I told him I was too tired. I told him I didn't feel well. I simply avoided him.

Sex has never been an easy topic for me to discuss, so when Dale and I first began squabbling over our sexual relationship, the last thing I was interested in was talking to someone else about it. It was my dirty little secret. I felt like I was the only woman in the world who would deny her disabled husband affection. What a terrible person I was!

Yet, at the same time, I felt no desire for Dale. Our relationship had changed from husband/wife to mother/child. It seemed nearly incestuous to make love to him.

The games we played might be comical to an outsider, but we were deadly serious. Bedtime was always a challenge. At first, because he tired easily, I could simply stay up until he went to bed. But bedtime grew later and later as we tried to outlast each other. Then I would wait until he was interested in a television show, and I would slip off to bed and pretend to be asleep when he got there. That didn't last long. He would simply wake me up, and I would get up while he stayed in bed angry and disappointed. I felt more and more guilty as the months went on.

It wasn't until a year or so of this game playing had gone by that another wife casually mentioned that she felt guilty that she could no longer be a wife to her disabled husband. Then it suddenly dawned on me that I wasn't the only spouse saying no. Hearing that was like someone had lifted 500 pounds off my shoulders.

Not everyone feels this way of course. Many men and women recover their intimate relationship after counseling or time. Some go on to raise families and be the best of friends and lovers. They accept the changes in their roles and in their personalities and are able to make the best of their lives. But, for others, the brain injury brings a stranger into the family, and redeveloping the husband/wife relationship is impossible.

Many wives say they can no longer be a sexual partner to man who is no longer the same man they married. The man who filled them with love and desire is gone—now he's more of a child than a husband. They take on an enormous amount of guilt in deciding to say no. Their husbands will certainly not understand, and society at large is critical. Once again the healthy spouse must learn to detach herself from the expectations of her spouse, her society and her own self-judgment. She can only give to her limits. Sometimes sex is more than she can give.

Sometimes time will make a difference. As the brain-injured person becomes more functional, the spouse may once again find him or her desirable. Many times a man and woman will find they can be loving without being sexual. Counseling may help resolve the guilt and misunderstanding. And sometimes the problem is never resolved.

Such problems are usually kept as secret as possible. Neither partner wants to discuss them with anyone else. The brain-injured spouse may not want anyone to know he or she is no longer desirable, and the healthy spouse doesn't want anyone to know that he or she isn't being a good spouse. But nearly every married couple who has to deal with brain injury will have some sexual problems. Please seek counseling if you are confronting this problem and facing overwhelming misunderstandings and exhausting yourselves with trying to reach an understanding. Another voice can give you much needed insight.

Dale and I finally reached a compromise. It is not an entirely agreeable arrangement, but it is a compromise of sorts. We decided to do without sexual intercourse for a time, which left me free to give more affection to Dale without feeling that I would be trapped, and he didn't have to deal with constant rejection on every front. As we learned to be friends, we gained back some emotional support that we both needed. We were once again able to have the warmth of that old friendship on occasion. It was a wonderful improvement over the conflict that went before.

Children

Children are by nature self-centered. They relate everything going on around them to their own feelings. But although they need and demand a great deal of attention, they are still very much a pawn of their families. They have no control over their own lives. They are totally dependent on what goes on inside the family home. That's why a brain injury in the family can be so devastating to a child. While adults may FEEL trapped, children ARE trapped. They have no way to get out of a dysfunctional family except to grow up and move away. And that takes a long time.

Kara, a talented creative writer, showed me a piece she had written for a class in which she described in scathing detail an incident in the kitchen with her father. She wrote about his criticism, the anger and shouting and her emotional response to it. Even though we could talk about her anger and her father's problems, she felt cheated. She felt that she had no father in

143

those formative years, and her anger at the father who still lived in our house never allowed her a chance to mourn. It is a big problem for children with a brain-injured parent. They feel they've been abandoned by that "good" parent, and yet there's a "bad" parent still hanging around; a person who is the center of everything that's wrong in the family.

It must seem to the children dealing with a brain-injured family member that everyone is in a hurry. We don't have much time to talk with them. They are often too young to understand the complex problems that their parent or sibling is experiencing, but they remain vulnerable to the giant mood swings and tensions in the household. Sometimes they are vulnerable to abuse as well. The healthy parent, or both parents, are so involved in the care of the brain-injured person that there is no time to explain anything to the child. Is it any wonder that so many of them turn to drugs, alcohol or food to dull their pain?

Living with a head-injured family member is difficult enough if you understand why things are like they are. But not only does the child lack this insight, but his parents are very likely caving in too. The people who control his life are out of control. All the role changes, the fighting, and the unpredictability of living with a head-injured person produce an environment of tension and apprehension.

Plus, this self-centered (and all kids are) young person has lost a great deal of contact with the very people who gave him support before. He may realize that he's being ignored because his brother or parent needs so much attention, but that doesn't make him need his share of attention any less. Chocolate makes him feel better. Or, if things get too bad, booze or drugs can sometimes dull the pain or make him feel euphoric.

What can you do to help even if you're going crazy yourself? Communicate. That means listening as well as talking. Your child may be thinking that something he did has caused all this trouble. As crazy as it seems, many of them believe this. As adults, we may not have an inkling of what's going on in this child's head. And while you're listening, remember not to say, "Oh, you shouldn't say that." Feelings aren't right or wrong. And if they can be said out loud, they aren't nearly as frightening as they are when they're locked up inside. Don't condemn their concerns as unfair or uncaring or selfish. If they can't tell you how bad they're feeling, they may begin to act it out by being rebellious and getting into trouble. As far as they can understand, tell them about brain injury and what effects it has. Help them learn to say, "It's not my problem," too. Try to make them understand that the behavior of the brain-injured person is not something they should take personally, even if they are attacked verbally or physically. It's not something they deserved.

Give them lots of love and affection. As you struggle with your many responsibilities, try to set up a few minutes each day with the healthy child to listen to his problems, hear about school or whatever. I often found those times in the car—on the way to somewhere else. On the way to an orthodontist appointment I heard that Mike was thinking about trying marijuana. Coming home from school I heard that one of Kara's classmates had had an abortion, and how upset Kara was that it had happened to someone only 13 years old. Those few moments of sharing kept our communication lines open throughout Mike's experiences with drugs, alcohol and rebellious friends. Kara and I have been able to talk about suicide and love and sex. We've talked about how their father acts and how it's not their fault that he has temper tantrums.

I try not to take sides, and I also try not to criticize the way they feel. I'm honest about my own resentments, and I've probably told them it's not their fault more than once every day. It helps. Just the other day, Mike saw that I was upset about something Dale had done and grinned at me.

"It's not your problem, Mom," he said.

Parents

Having lost the privilege of driving because of his brain injury, Dale was determined to have some independence—the freedom to come and go when I couldn't be there to serve as his driver.

A friend helped him pick out a mountain bike. We hoped that the sturdy bike with its wide tires and many gears would offset his clumsiness and lack of balance, and allow him to ride the five miles into town in safety. At first, he rode the bike up and down the dirt lane from our house to the busy street. As he got better, he rode farther and farther from home. Each time he pedaled out onto our busy street, where the traffic whizzes by at speeds of 50 miles an hour or more, I would grit my teeth and hope that my heart would keep beating. It was frightening for me, but for his parents it was an exercise in panic. If he was late, they would worry about what might have happened to him. If he was tired when he started home, they would call to tell me. Sometimes they would convince him to let them drive him home.

Many parents would have fought hard to keep their child from making that bicycle ride, particularly after the first time he was struck by a car. But having raised him to be independent and assertive, Dale's parents had the courage to allow him to continue to live that way even though they had to constantly curb their own fear as they encouraged him. It wasn't easy.

All a parent's natural protective instincts come to full alert when his or her child is brain-injured. Parents will fight for their child's recovery with every resource at their disposal. They will quit their jobs to help with therapy. They will fight anyone who says their child can't recover. They will search out whatever treatment offers hope. Or they may pray for their child to die rather than have him live as a "vegetable."

They will do almost anything to insure the least pain for their child. Occasionally parents will protect their child so well that he will not be able to develop coping skills of his own. Afraid of another injury, parents will not allow the risk-taking that leads to bigger and better victories for the brain-injured person. Just as some healthy children never learn to get along with their peers, a brain-injured person who is overprotected never relearns the skills of living in society. He never is allowed to reach, fall and pick himself up again—a basic part of life.

Just as they must let their healthy child drive the car by himself when he is old enough and trained, parents must let their brain-injured child take on new challenges for which he is prepared. Only then can the child continue to grow.

Of course, many brain-injured children and adults never recover fully. That leads to another dilemma for parents. Always at the back of their minds is the question, "What will happen to this child when I can no longer care for him?" If the immediate family is willing to take on the care, this lessens the fear for parents, but many family members are not. They've been watching the demands placed on their parents and they don't wish to subject their own families to that kind of stress.

Fortunately, transitional housing and other housing options are becoming more available for brain-injured people. Many new facilities are under development. But it will still be difficult for parents to turn their child over to strangers. It is another risk that parents must take in order to give their child a better life in the future.

Jigsaw Puzzle

Dealing with head injury is undeniably the biggest challenge I've ever faced. I've wept and raged and sometimes have been so depressed that life didn't seem worth living. Sometimes I felt like I hated the whole world. I was convinced I was the only person who had ever suffered so terribly even though I knew people who have suffered much more. It has been a long and difficult battle.

But good things have come from this tragedy. We have learned much about life and about ourselves in our years of dealing with head injury. Despite what we've been through, our family is still close and loving. We know each other much better than we did before. We are stronger. We are more compassionate. We have a confidence that can only come from facing a difficult obstacle and overcoming it. Yes, we have scars, but we also have our medals of valor.

Out of the chaos that enveloped us, we have built stronger foundations for our lives. Each member of our family carries a new knowledge inside him or herself that breeds confidence. I am not afraid of what might happen anymore. I guess that sounds a little strange. Now that I know that tragedy can strike my family at any time, one might expect me to be more fearful. But I'm just realistic. The most important change for me is that I have an inner peace that I had never felt before. I have gained a great deal of knowledge from this experience, and I've learned how to use that knowledge for good. But most importantly, I've learned that life is not a game in which the goal is to get everything you want—a game where controlling the outcome is everything. Life is to be lived—with all its pain, struggle, joy, anger and pleasure. I can't truly enjoy living if I'm constantly watching over my shoulder for something to go wrong. The sky might fall in, but being fearful about it will only rob me of the joy I could have been experiencing before it fell. Pain is no less a part of life than pleasure, and we can often learn just as much from it.

Before, when I thought Dale was being an insensitive jerk, I couldn't see that he might just be human. Fearful that I wasn't going to have a happy marriage, I didn't allow myself to see the decent, kind man behind the annoying actions. I focused at first on changing his actions so that I got what I wanted. Head injury has taught me that trying to control the personality and actions of anyone but myself is absolute nonsense. As a result, I have given my children more freedom to become their own creations, and we are very good friends. I have given Dale the freedom and time to grow as much as possible without pressure to change. And for the first time in many years, we are friends again.

I cherish these friendships. They are one of the most beautiful parts of my life. I can go forward from here, not embittered, but empowered by my experience with brain injury.

Dale used to be a perpetually angry man. With his perfectionist personality, he found the world a chaotic and uncomfortable place. He waged war against sloppiness and inconsistency and was disapproving of most of his fellow human beings because they were less than perfect. He was also very harsh on his own imperfections.

I'm not sure when he began to see other people as imperfect but acceptable anyway. I believe it came as he learned to accept himself in this new imperfect state. (He still tries to change them though.) His outlook on life is so different, so forgiving, that I often stop and stare when he voices some recently changed, gentle opinion. He no longer sees life as such a burden. He has come to enjoy it in all its imperfection and with all its challenges.

My children too are strong and hopeful in their approach to life. They look forward to their respective futures, knowing there will be failures and obstacles, yet feeling confident that their lives will be enjoyable.

We could have emerged from this experience with resentment, anger and bitterness, but we didn't. While I would never choose to experience brain injury if I were given a choice, living with its challenges has enriched our family. I am grateful for the friends and family who helped us get through the experience. Their love and support have made the difference between victory and failure. I have a much deeper faith in the goodness of men and women now.

One of the things I found from listening to many head injury families who seem to be coping well is that they don't look backward. They don't brood over the brain injury. Perhaps it is that acceptance we all must reach. Yes, it was supposed to happen to someone else, but this time it happened to us. Now it's time to move forward.

I hope the information in this book will help you cope with the problems brought on by a head injury in your family. The people who shared their stories with me deserve a lot of credit for their honesty. It isn't always easy to share secrets to help someone else.

Most of us have seen our lives get easier as time progressed after brain injury. That is the hope we offer you. While the problems never go away, you can learn to deal with them just as you once learned to deal with dirty laundry or changing a tire.

Your local support group can be an invaluable aid in helping you cope. There are many contacts listed in the back of the book. Reach out on the Internet. Reach out to your medical professionals, your minister, your psychologist. They won't know that you need them until you say so.

You are not alone.

Dale's Story

As shared with our friend Dudley Lynch, president of Brain Technologies Corporation

It is not a vicious limp, but if you watch Dale Maxwell approach, you will notice that one leg lags a little behind the pace set by the other. It is enough to tell you that something significant is out of kilter for this 43-year-old former electrical engineer.

There is much about Dale, however, that is not so cut and dried. It is not simple to decide what you really know and think about this man who five years ago made a bargain with God and, when it appeared he had lost, decided not so much with bitterness but with resignation that there had been no one to bargain with. Lately, though, he's thought a lot about bargaining with God, and he wonders about his prior audacity.

For the first time since his head injury—caused by a stroke during surgery for an aneurysm in his brain—Dale has agreed to talk with a non-family member about who he is, where he has been and where he sees himself going.

He arrives in faded jeans and a trim blue-over-white golf shirt. He wears no socks beneath his scoured brown sneakers. His gold wedding band is in place. And his heavy digital watch has the appearance of a piece that has kept time in sometimes strenuous circumstances: it's scraped, battered and banged—to some extent, you might say, like its owner.

We are about to spend three hours together, hours that will fly for us both, and when we are finished Dale will volunteer that it has been the second-best conversation of the past five years.

(The best time of his new life was at a Christmas party three years before, hours during which he forgot that he was a man missing part of his brain, and he talked and talked and talked.) But as we begin, he confesses that he has dreaded this moment of attempting to tell his story. "I'm scared," he says. Then he corrects himself. "No, I'm nervous."

The quality of his memory constantly frustrates and inhibits Dale, and there are other impediments created by having part of your brain removed and other parts of it die. But even a cursory examination of his physical appearance testifies to the fact that this is not a man without careful personal standards. His mahogany hair is slightly flecked with gray but impeccably barbered, and he has combed it meticulously. Behind the carefully groomed strands on the left side sits the reminder of a sizable incision. At that point, Dale's head falls inward in a shallow "v," and the downward-curving scimitar of a scar emerges from his hair like a small canyon peeking from beneath chaparral bushes. Through this long-healed slash the brain surgeon entered his head five years ago and altered his life, and his family's lives, forever.

He has some memories of his hospitalizations. "I can remember getting up," he chuckles, "before I was even supposed to. But I needed to go to the bathroom, so I got up and went." As he talks, there are frequent pauses in Dale's speech, and as he searches for those memories and for the words to recount them, he fidgets, sometimes squinting or rubbing his knuckles or pulling at his ear. "But I don't remember very much. I can imagine how a nurse would take a spoon…well, that's all they had, a spoon…and I can imagine how she would feed me." At this point, he stops. "I'm getting nervous," he says.

Would taking some deep breaths help?

"No," he says with some feeling, and he laughs. He understands that what we have come together to talk about are things that might be helpful to others involved in a head injury experience, but he expresses doubt about where to begin. "It's too broad," he says of the idea of drawing on his experiences to help others.

Fair enough. So let's forget about helping a listening world and talk just about him. What does he need? What could be done to help him? It is a question that gives him an opening to say something he wants to talk about: this book that Marilyn Colter, his wife of twenty-two years, has written, a book that just days before she read to him, word for word.

"When I read this book, when Marilyn read the book to me, I had no idea that there was so much turmoil around my injury." (During this sentence, Dale halted three or four times, not so much to collect his thoughts as his words. The damage to his brain is in the area where language is processed, and for him to "frame" his thoughts is much easier than to express them. Each of his pauses was brief—perhaps two or three seconds. From this point on, your interviewer will make no notes of pauses.)

"I thought that they (his wife and two children) were picking on me. So what I would do is that I would trap myself in a chair, and I would make that place my turf. I would wash all dishes that they would bring to me, but I wouldn't touch dishes that were not brought into my domain. I felt that was a reasonable approach to what I was doing, and then after I heard her read the story, I realized that, boy, I was really wrong. And now it seems funny, but I do all the dishes."

Dale's eyes are glistening, and he has trouble for a moment finding the breath to speak.

"I love Marilyn. I love Kara (his daughter)."

A tiny sob escapes, and we stop for a time.

"And I love Mike (his son.) I do love them…Can I have that question again, please, because I am kind of wandering, and I haven't answered that question yet."

The question was, "What do you need at the moment from your family?"

The high tide of emotion passes, and Dale continues:

"Mike, he gives more. But Kara, I cannot deal with. I think she loves, but she kind of hides it from me. I don't think she can. I don't think it's bad, except it's not happening. I don't know. Probably if I would talk to her about it, but I really don't think she would listen to me. I wouldn't get any feelings about it. I would go for it and I would discuss it and I would come out zero. And I think that's the best I could do. And so, well, that's Kara."

He returns to Marilyn and his love for her. "That's a new twist," he says. He exhales audibly, part laughter, partly a sigh of – what—wonder, surprise, delight, relief? "Since I read her article (book) or when she read it to me—it's not that I didn't love her, it isn't the same way as I love her now. I don't know how I'm going to say this."

Maybe, he hears, it is just best to call it the way it is.

He repeats the words. "Call it the way it is. I love her…call it the way it is?…and before I just kind of loved her. Oh yes. I talked to her about going to a counselor because I felt that she needed it, that obviously she needed counseling, and we ought to go to counseling. Then after she read the book to me, I saw that it is not necessary. Because now then I can push a lot of blame on

156

myself. And I think that is good that we had that book written. It meant a lot to me."

The book could have been read to him many months earlier. Had he ever considered doing this?

"Yeah, but I was kind of afraid to ask for it."

He wasn't ready to hear it?

"Yes, or I would have imagined that Marilyn would not be willing to read it. I imagined all sorts of wicked things. Then, my father was going to read it to me when we went up to the cabin up Poudre River. He was going to read it after we arrived at the house up there. And he never did. I didn't ask him because I guess I was afraid that he really didn't want to read it. But it wasn't so bad. I'm glad that the book was read to me. I'm glad you (the book's publisher) made me have it read to me."

We both laugh, enjoying the happy aftermath produced by having been partners in such an act of collusion.

Dale's interviewer notes that he has known him for three of the five years since the brain surgery. We talk about what a difference three years can make. Dale appears pleased, appears satisfied, with the idea that he, the new Dale, has matured. The "old Dale" had a reputation for a low flash point—for flying off the handle, for having inflexible opinions. What, he is asked, are things and circumstances that make him angry now?

He grins. "I guess I'm, I'm easy-going because I'm not ever mad. I think I've been taught to hide it. I'm not sure now that I'm ever mad at all except that court thing (he and his wife have been embroiled for months in a court action growing out of a traffic accident). So I'm not sure when I'm mad and when I'm happy, and I'm not sure I can draw a line between them. And I'm kind of glad that it's working that way because it gives me a better dealing with Marilyn. They come, and they go."

It's spring in Colorado—springtime in the Rockies!—and he has planted a garden. Yesterday, he says, he used a Rotor-Tiller to break up the soil in his garden and that of his brother-in-law, Steve.

He's always loved a garden, only before his surgery, Marilyn always planted and tilled and harvested the family's garden, he recalls. "And I loved it. I'd go in and have corn-on-the-cob and all, but it was all her hands. Now, it is all my hands. I've already got some tomatoes—I've got them indoors. And I'm going to plant them. And I've already planted, not in the garden but in the same place that my tomatoes are planted, some hot peppers, some—oh, gee, all I can think of is tamales…"

Jalapeno?

"Yes, some jalapeno pepper plants. And I've got some regular garden peppers, bell peppers. And I imagine that I will plant some peas and beans and onions and carrots and squash."

And how about his cooking?

"I'm cooking my own foods because I am vegetarian now. This happened about two or three months ago. I was getting fat. I was getting fat, and I didn't like it. I liked it last year when I was skinny because whenever I rode on my bike every other day to …it starts with an 's'…Salvation Army, and I was cooking for them. I was making desserts. Mostly, I was making their cookies. And then I left that because it was hard to ride that far (about five miles each way) without getting killed. Almost every other day I would get hit by a car, and they would just keep on going. So I had to cancel that."

158

Following that, Dale says, he volunteered to help at a greenhouse, potting plants and such. He liked working with the soils and the plants, and he might still be there if not for the fact that he gave in to a desire to start his own woodworking shop. By the time he got it going, though, the Colorado winter had set in. His "shop of sorts" is difficult to heat. But now that summer is nearing, he admits to thoughts of getting back to the woodworking. "I've got to, I've got to," he says with some authority. "Because I need something to do." But does he? He thinks for a moment about what he's involved in. His garden. His cooking. And he volunteers that he is spending a lot of time at what he calls reading. Listening to cassette tapes of narrators reading the text of books.

At the moment, he is "reading" a book written in the early 1930s, a book about herbs. "I'm liking it because it also covers recipes," Dale says. "And there's another book that I got—I can't remember the name of it. But it was written about 1966, and it's about healing with thoughts. I guess that's what I would call it. I'm only about halfway through that. Being halfway through it there is still a lot to go. And I think that I would get 20 percent of it from listening to it the first time. Maybe less, but I would guess 20 percent. I've got to get my ability to recall better. And I think I can do it if I am going to read books because…I haven't any idea what I was going to say."

Twice in the past few moments, he has used the word "healing." Does that mean that he has launched himself on a self-improvement program, and if so, what all is involved?

"I like the healing by—what did I say?—thought, I really like that," he replies. "There's no set time when it is available to me. The timing is mine. And so now if I'm going to heal myself by just meditating or whatever, I wouldn't be losing time. I wouldn't be losing a thing. Now, what was the question again?"

Self-improvement. Meditating.

"I'm not meditating yet, but I'm learning the way to meditate," he says. "He (the author of the book he is listening to) has discovered three ways to meditate. I'm going to get them all messed up. But he said you want to come in and you want to sit down and relax. And he says then you are going to feel your arms get heavy. It's going to get heavy. And then you are going to feel your other arm get heavy. And then you are going to feel something else. So what I want to do is I would like to find out why this arm (he indicates his right arm) is so cold. This arm and leg are ice cold. And I would like to switch, to heat this one. And I believe that I can. And then if it is heated up by meditating on it, then what would happen if I tapped the best side of my mind and I have recovered the use of my legs? I have now healed this portion of my body, and I think that this is possible."

In suggesting that his right arm and leg were "ice cold," wasn't Dale simply describing how they seemed to him? To someone else's touch, their temperature would not be noticeably different than that of his left arm and leg, correct? Dale answers by extending both arms. And when his companion of the moment touches the two of them, unquestionably, the right arm is several degrees cooler than the left.

He begins, "When I had my operation…" But he doesn't quite know how to explain.

Blood pressure, blood flow?

"Yes," he says. "It's not high enough. When I was in the hospital I had a stroke—stroke? –yes, stroke, and I think it affected my arm and my leg to the point that it is now. And I have never gained that limb at all. It affects my walk when I'm tired. I drag it (his leg). I guess that is my problem, entirely. The stroke, I believe. Well, if I'm writing a letter, it will take me longer than it should to write a paragraph. And then I have to remember what it was I wrote. And I have to go back, and I have to read it again. And then I might go long and write another one. And then I have to go back and read them both. And this is four hours later. So it is hard for me to write. Anything. My speaking, my speech, my reading, I think it could be about thirty words a minute, and that is slow. Thirty words a minute, it is not nearly fast enough. It doesn't compare to a hundred words a minute."

So he thinks he can improve his memory. And he's working to raise the temperatures of his right arm and leg. And he's thinking about other things to do to occupy his time. What of the future? What does he *want* to do?

"Future?" Dale repeats. He finds the question a difficult one. He thinks about it for the better part of a minute.

"My ideal is to go back to work healed, go back to Kodak and (they) gladly put me back to work, and that is not going to happen. So I guess I haven't found out what it is that I'm good at. So I imagine I will go back and make my wood projects, and I will come to some thoughts of what I could do. Because I really don't know now. Because, yeah, I have no idea what I am good at, because I am not good at woodworking because it's going to take me time. How am I going to say this? If I charged by the hour, it would be very, very costly. So I am doing it mostly just because I want to do it. That was how it started—because I want to do it."

He describes a graduation gift he started many months ago and realizes with something of a start, that he must finish it soon because the intended recipient is graduating and that helps him make the point: if he was being paid the minimum wage for this project, he'd need to sell it for about $85. But actually, he says it is worth only about $15. "It's okay, because it gives me money to play with, and it gives me something to do, and that's okay. But I don't think I could afford to let it go and leave it at that. So I have to find something that I can do which I can do on my own and won't be affected by the time that is needed. And I have problems with that—trying to define what it is that I'm going to do. I don't have any plans made. And that sounds really dull, and I don't want to sound dull, but it's just that I haven't found anything yet."

But he's looking?

"Well, I'm interested," he replies. "I imagine that reading the book (the cassette tapes he's listening to) will give me some ideas."

We take a break, and Dale reaches for his coffee cup. Prior to his surgery, he drank coffee incessantly, beginning with breakfast and continuing through the day. But the surgery changed that, he says. He will still drink it but without the craving that was once there. The same is true, he says, with alcoholic beverages, which were once a problem for him.

"I don't drink (alcohol) at all anymore," he volunteers. "Not because I've sworn off. I guess it's because my memory is failing or whatever, but I got a bottle of wine which is about 2 percent (a very weak volume of alcohol) that was left over from a party. And one bottle will last me forever. And I haven't been drinking beer, but I will if I get a chance. At a party, I will drink two beers or three, maybe. But three, with my alcohol consumption (tolerance being what it is) will make me high. And I've got hard liquor, and it's around the house, but out of five years I have gotten to where I will fix myself a drink one week and then forget it. I'll have a beer. But I don't get drunk."

Next, we speak about religion. Before his surgery, did he consider himself religious? And, how about now?

He and Marilyn have friends—and he mentions them by name—who by his standards are very religious.

"And we started on the trail that is religion, and we met with the pastor of the Timnath Church (a small town near Fort Collins, Colorado) until the pastor died kind of suddenly. We were in that church with (the friends he mentioned). And it was a good thing for us. And then Marilyn's father died. And shortly after that, the pastor died, and we haven't been back to church. Oh, we'd go on Easter or something. But then we stopped getting invited because of my injury. Oh, they would still invite us, but…well, you see, I had it figured out perfectly. There was going to be a God, or there was going to be no God. And I was going to find out one way or another. As soon as the operation was through, the answer was that there was no God because you're injured. I had made myself a bet that if God's there, I would get through the operation excellent. And if there was not God there, I might fail. My failure was less than I expected because I wasn't dead. But He still failed.

"Now I am not quite sure of that whole thing. I haven't been to church in three or four years."

What is it that he is no longer quite sure of? Will he tell us more?

"I'm not sure that I'm allowed to question that," he replies. "I'm not sure that if I was God, I would even listen to me. Because Dale Maxwell had his chance, and he blew it. It's hard for me to read, and it's hard for me to remember, and it's hard for me to do anything that would support a religion. Now, most of the songs that are coming out of Christmas I can sing because I can just remember them. But not much else is correct about my memory. So I'm not sure that I have found out the truth, or if I'm still in the middle. I don't know where I am going to find it out, but I imagine by reading."

Dale is reminded that his Christian God has been portrayed as a forgiving God. Is it possible that this God might forgive Dale Maxwell for doubting Him if Dale Maxwell wanted it?

"Well, that might be the case," he answers.

The surgeon who entered his brain—how does he feel about him, Dale is asked. Any anger, any regrets?

"No, I imagine that he did the best that he could," Dale answers. He adds nothing more.

He has had a speech therapist, one named Ann, whom he enjoyed very much. "She would walk an extra mile," he explains. "She came out to my house once, as soon as I got the computer. I got some tapes (audio cassette tapes,) and she wanted to hear them, and she wanted feedback. And she would do that. That was just her style. And my training was going great. But she moved."

And he did not replace her. Had she stayed in Colorado, does he think his recovery process would have progressed faster?

"I'm not sure I would have made any more, but I would have been trying. She gathered a group of us. She wanted us to sit down and discuss things once a week, and I liked that Richard and Michelle. And Craig, and myself. I think we all liked it."

How about friends? Did he lose any after his surgery?

He answered immediately and candidly. "I have a hard time making friends," he says. "I did go to breakfast every Friday with the fellows who were working with me when I was working at Kodak. I've been going to that regularly until two months ago, and then I quit because it didn't feel like it was fitting any more. And I didn't talk to them; I just quit it. They were good to me, and they'd be talking at a rapid rate, and I could make out maybe 10 percent of what they were saying, and it never got any better than that. The last breakfast we had was with our wives, and it was on Sunday. And then I kind of quit it. And I'm not sure I'm going to quit it permanently. I would like to get together and say hello to them once a month or something. I've got to get myself together and give them a call. But most of my friends are gone, and I don't even remember enough to state their names."

Names escape him, but he says he can remember many of their faces. He has about six or eight friends, he says—and he names them. With some, he can remember only their first names. With others, he can remember full names and names of their spouses.

It takes only a moment, and he says, "That's all. Everybody else is kind of acquaintances now."

Obviously, Dale's world has vastly changed. Some things he simply can't do any longer. Some things he can do, but perhaps not as well. But are there some things he can do better than before his surgery?

"I'm much better at verbalizing—at speaking," he says. But even as he says it, he says it haltingly, and some clarification is required: does he mean that he thinks he is better now than before at expressing his most deeply felt and held sentiments?

"Yes, I think that's right, but if you were to ask the guys that I was having breakfast with, I imagine they would say that there is no change. Because I haven't changed much as they can be aware of. But I can speak better, and I can get my point across. I imagine I can. This reading I think is fantastic. If I had only known what the number to call was (at the Library for the Blind) and that they would help me with anything. If I had only known that before, I would have been ahead of where I am now."

And where is he now, his interviewer wonders but, deciding to keep his own counsel, doesn't ask.

But then, perhaps Dale has already answered.

In the middle, he'd said. In the middle.

He's alive, not dead.

He's a more patient man now than before.

A man with hope.

Hoping to improve his memory.

Hoping to heal himself.

Hoping to discover what he is good at.

Believing he is loved.

Loving others himself.

Knowing things have changed.

Drastically.

Forever.

But acting out of the assumption that the God he once sought to bargain with may not be done with him even yet.

A Final Word from the Author

There are a lot of questions that go unanswered between family members in our situation. Others are only half-answered, and sometimes we're not sure we believe the answers that we get. But after reading what Dale has to say about his struggle, I see something new growing inside his mind and heart. I was not sure I'd seen it before. I had wished for it. I had tried to manufacture it. I had tried to give it to him.

Hope.

He is beginning to move his focus from the past to the future.

Like most family members of head-injured people, I try to keep the joy I feel at this new recognition under control. I don't want this pleasure to be dashed against some coming failure, so I temper it with common sense and a pragmatic approach.

But, God, it feels so good!

We have reached a turning point of sorts. Like the pioneers who crossed the Great Plains, we have survived the worst. We can see where we have been, and although we haven't quite reached our destination, we can see it on the horizon. We can look back and see just how difficult it was to get to this point and marvel at our strength.

The other day, Dale came in from the yard where he had been surveying the newly budding trees and flowers.

"Maybe I was meant to be handicapped," he said to me.

"What?" I couldn't believe he could say such a thing.

"No. What I mean is that I love being here and seeing things grow and just being alive. I never used to let myself enjoy things. I was too busy."

Perhaps God is still fulfilling his side of the bargain.

Note to the revised edition

A few years after this book was written, Dale told me he wanted a divorce. He wanted to free us all from brain injury, he said. I believe he could no longer live with the constant reminders of who he had been before and the constant tension of the changing family roles. With the kids in college and embarking on lives of their own, we parted amicably. Dale remarried and then divorced and made a home for himself alone. He volunteered at the local hospital and made friends in his church. He is currently on a mission to help the homeless in San Francisco.

Ironically, in 2003, Dale's brother was brain-injured during surgery and Dale moved to California to be near him and help him with his recovery. At dinner, before he left for California, Dale told me that he hoped to be able to help his brother handle the anger that comes along with brain injury in a better way than Dale had done, and spare his family some of the pain that we had gone through.

Dale has come so far, lost so much, gained so much and helped us learn so much. Our family is strong but changed. Although we all bear scars, we have healed well and celebrate life. We hope the same for you.

If you want to learn more about brain injury, the Internet will deliver. Please use reliable sites of hospitals and researchers to help you get the best information. What a gift this has been for brain injury families. Start with sites like MedLine, the Mayo Clinic and Wounded Warriors.

51898391R00097

Made in the USA
Middletown, DE
05 July 2019